RADICAL
AUTHENTICITY

BEING THE CHURCH
IN THE WORLD

3

DR. WILLIE JOUBERT

Tellwell Talent
www.tellwell.ca

ISBN
978-0-2288-4419-8 (Hardcover)
978-0-2288-4418-1 (Paperback)
978-0-2288-4420-4 (eBook)

CONTENTS

Acknowledgements.. 1

Introduction.. 3

Faith Comes by Hearing 7

A Kingdom Mindset 19

Seeing with Kingdom Eyes... 28

A Fruitful Vine... 42

Compelling Love in Action 62

The King's Resources 83

Servant Leaders 104

Church in the New Testament 133

The Remnant... 169

Being The Church 189

Epilogue... 215

About the Author... 217

ACKNOWLEDGEMENTS

At the end of writing this book I want to express my sincere gratitude to a number of people.

A special thanks to Norman with whom I have been privileged and also forced to journey for a while. Thanks for the input and challenging thoughts and for helping me to ask questions and seek answers. I hope never to travel the same road again, but will not have missed it for anything in the world.

Also special thanks to my wife, Eda. You have walked this walk with me and I do not think anyone else will ever realize how difficult it was at times. Your presence and support have been an incredible inspiration and I thank the Lord for you.

I need to express my thanks to the many who walked with us and in radical and authentic ways touched our lives and illustrated The Way. You have been and are true friends and brothers and sisters in Christ. A special word of thanks to those who have seen the Kingdom vision and were willing to walk out of the traditional comfort zones of the established North American church model to walk in radical authenticity and to be the church, particularly the believers in Georgetown and others scattered throughout South Western Ontario. May God bless you and add to your numbers!

Finally, and most importantly, I want to again express my gratitude to my Lord, Jesus, to the Father who loved this world enough to send him and to the Holy Spirit who has given us so much and opened the truth of the Scriptures in fresh and amazing ways during this time.

INTRODUCTION

On October 31, 1517, a monk by the name of Martin Luther radically changed the course of history when he nailed 95 theses on the door of a church in Wittenberg, Germany. Many diverse streams flowed into what is known as the Protestant Reformation, but this act was a decisive turning point. In terms of Jesus' picture in Luke 5:37 the old wineskin of Roman Catholicism split wide open as the new wine was poured out. It could not and never would be able to contain the new wine of the gospel. The darkness that came into the church was shattered as the light of God's Word began to shine and people who were kept in darkness for lack of knowledge were able to read the Word for themselves in their own language. Many truths, lost and buried for centuries under layers of ungodly traditions, were recovered and new foundations were laid for the church.

As we enter the new millennium, the Third Day of our Lord, there is a new Reformation on the horizon that will shatter every wineskin of the existing church as much and more than the Protestant Reformation. Just like it happened in Luther's day, there are already many streams flowing and no one will stop or contain this flow. Again, God is pouring out the new wine and the wineskins cannot contain this wine. The foundations of the church are cracked and patching the cracks won't work, as I described in the book "Restoring the broken foundations." **The key issue that was never addressed by the Protestant Reformation involves the priesthood of the believer.** While that was recognized in theory, it was ignored in the practice of the church. The Reformation did not change the Christianized version of the Levitical priesthood, which followed the conversion of the emperor Constantine in the fourth century. As a result, the church as we know it in the Western world functions on the basis of the Levitical model of the priesthood. However, the Scriptures are very clear that in Jesus this model was abolished and replaced by a new order, the order of Melchizedek. As we move into this Third Day the wineskins of the churches will break, because the order of Melchizedek cannot be contained in the current structures. In this Third Day God is calling ordinary people out of the Levitical order churches through the gate of control into the wilderness of the world to be his church, as I wrote in the book "Ordinary People Extraordinary Royal Priests."

God is calling out a remnant to walk through the gate and out of the comfort zones of the four walls and endless programs that achieve nothing but preserve the status quo. God is calling out his unfaithful wife into the desert to allure her and betroth her forever (Hosea 2:14-23). He is calling out those who are tired of the heavy burdens of religious tradition to enter into his Sabbath rest (Hebrews 4). He is seeking the many who are wandering like sheep without a shepherd, for they have suffered in the four walls of the fold and could not take it any more. He is calling forth those with an apostolic anointing who are able to see the vision of his heart for his church. He is calling those who are driven to explore the new lands and cross into the unknown. He is seeking those with eyes that can see the desert of life in the world changed as streams of living waters are released by their presence in the workplace. He is calling those who can see the divine Kingdom established in the world through the power of his Spirit in their lives and who do not want to hide their light under a bowl. **In a word: He is calling out a people who are prepared to live lives with a Radical Authenticity.**

To set the stage let us simply listen to the words of our Lord recorded in Luke 14:25-35:

Large crowds were traveling with Jesus, and turning to them he said: "If anyone comes to me and does not hate his father and mother, his wife and children, his brothers and sisters - yes, even his own life - he cannot be my disciple. And anyone who does not carry his cross and follow me cannot be my disciple.

Suppose one of you wants to build a tower. Will he not first sit down and estimate the cost to see if he has enough money to complete it? For if he lays the foundation and is not able to finish it, everyone who sees it will ridicule him, saying, 'This fellow began to build and was not able to finish.'

Or suppose a king is about to go to war against another king. Will he not first sit down and consider whether he is able with ten thousand men to oppose the one coming against him with twenty thousand? If he is not able, he will send a delegation while the other is still a long way off and will ask for terms of peace. <u>In the same way, any of you who does not give up everything he has cannot be my disciple.</u> Salt is good, but if it loses its saltiness, how can it be made salty again? It is fit neither for the soil nor for the manure pile; it is thrown out."

"He who has ears to hear, let him hear."

Incidentally, that is the very place where the journey of faith begins. The first step is simply to listen and hear the voice of God. Let us begin by doing just that.

FAITH COMES BY HEARING

The author of the Letter to the Hebrews began this letter with the following words, Hebrews 1::1-2:

In the past God spoke to our forefathers through the prophets at many times and in various ways, but in these last days he has spoken to us by his Son, whom he appointed heir of all things, and through whom he made the universe.

Now when we consider that the Son, *Jesus Christ, is the same yesterday and today and forever* (Hebrews 13:8), then this Jesus is speaking to his church today! As we enter into this Third Day the Lord has a very specific message for his church. He is challenging us to be the church in the world and to walk in radical authenticity as a way of life. However, much of the church is like the Hebrews who struggled to hear and understand as we read in Hebrews 5:10-14:

He was called by God as High Priest "according to the order of Melchizedek," of whom we have much to say, and it is hard to explain, since you have become dull of hearing. For though by this time you ought to be teachers, you need someone to teach you again the first principles of the oracles of God; and you have come to need milk and not solid food. For everyone who partakes only of milk is unskilled in the word of righteousness, for he is a babe. But solid food belongs to those who are of full age, that is, those who by reason of use have their senses exercised to discern both good and evil. (NKJV)

Let us take a fresh look at this man Jesus and his message. When John penned his gospel, he began by stating that the man Jesus is the very essence of the Word of God. We read the following in John 1:1-18:

<u>In the beginning was the Word, and the Word was with God, and the Word was God. He was with God in the beginning.</u> Through him all things were made; without him nothing was made that has been made. In him was life, and that life was the light of men. The light shines in the darkness, but the darkness has not understood it. There came a man who was sent from God; his name was John. He came as a witness to testify concerning that light, so that through him all men might believe. He himself was not the light; he came only as a witness to the light. The true light that gives light to every man was coming into the world. <u>He was in the world, and though the world was made through him, the world did not recognize him. He came to that which was his own, but his own did not receive him.</u> Yet to all who received him, to those who believed in his name, he gave the right to become children of God - children born not of natural descent, nor of human decision or a husband's will, but born of God. The Word became flesh and made his dwelling among us. We

have seen his glory, the glory of the One and Only, who came from the Father, full of grace and truth. (NIV)

Thus, to hear Jesus was to hear God. To listen to him was to listen to God. Yet, right at the outset John wrote that even though Jesus came to his own people, they did not receive him! In fact, as the story continues, we find that very clearly stated, e.g. in John 5 Jesus spoke about himself and then said in verses 31-40:

"If I testify about myself, my testimony is not valid. There is another who testifies in my favor, and I know that his testimony about me is valid. You have sent to John and he has testified to the truth. Not that I accept human testimony; but I mention it that you may be saved. John was a lamp that burned and gave light, and you chose for a time to enjoy his light. I have testimony weightier than that of John. <u>For the very work that the Father has given me to finish, and which I am doing, testifies that the Father has sent me. And the Father who sent me has himself testified concerning me. You have never heard his voice nor seen his form, nor does his word dwell in you, for you do not believe the one he sent. You diligently study the Scriptures because you think that by them you possess eternal life. These are the Scriptures that testify about me, yet you refuse to come to me to have life.</u>"

Note that Jesus said they diligently studied the Scriptures, yet refused to accept his word and refused to recognize that he is the very one revealed in the Scriptures! They heard every word he said – yet they did not hear at all, for they did not accept the person of Jesus and his message. In fact, the startling reality about this matter is that those, whom we should have expected to understand, were often the very ones who heard, but chose to reject the message. On the other side we see that the unlikely ones did hear him! When the seventy-two sent out by Jesus returned and reported how they ministered in his name, we read in Luke 10:17-24:

The seventy-two returned with joy and said, "Lord, even the demons submit to us in your name."

He replied, "I saw Satan fall like lightning from heaven. I have given you authority to trample on snakes and scorpions and to overcome all the power of the enemy; nothing will harm you. However, do not rejoice that the spirits submit to you, but rejoice that your names are written in heaven."

At that time Jesus, full of joy through the Holy Spirit, said, "I praise you, Father, Lord of heaven and earth, because you have hidden these things from the wise and learned, and revealed them to little children. Yes, Father, for this was your good pleasure.

"All things have been committed to me by my Father. No one knows who the Son is except the Father, and no one knows who the Father is except the Son and those to whom the Son chooses to reveal him."

Then he turned to his disciples and said privately, "Blessed are the eyes that see what you see. For I tell you that many prophets and kings wanted to see what you see but did not see it, and to hear what you hear but did not hear it."

The most unlikely ones heard him and received the message and walked in authority, but the wise and learned saw him and listened to him and never walked in faith. Today in many parts of the world the least likely "little ones" walk and operate in the authority of Jesus, while many a graduate reject the message of the Lord. The church in the Western world is the least productive and least effective church in the world! We have all the scholarship and resources, great buildings with all the equipment to run the latest programs, but we do not effectively impact our society.

Before we become too defensive, let us read the well-known parable in Matthew 13:1-23:

That same day Jesus went out of the house and sat by the lake. Such large crowds gathered around him that he got into a boat and sat in it, while all the people stood on the shore. Then he told them many things in parables, saying: "A farmer went out to sow his seed. As he was scattering the seed, some fell along the path, and the birds came and ate it up. Some fell on rocky places, where it did not have much soil. It sprang up quickly, because the soil was shallow. But when the sun came up, the plants were scorched, and they withered because they had no root. Other seed fell among thorns, which grew up and choked the plants. Still other seed fell on good soil, where it produced a crop-a hundred, sixty or thirty times what was sown. He who has ears, let him hear."

The disciples came to him and asked, "Why do you speak to the people in parables?"

He replied, "The knowledge of the secrets of the kingdom of heaven has been given to you, but not to them. Whoever has will be given more, and he will have an abundance. Whoever does not have, even what he has will be taken from him. This is why I speak to them in parables:

"Though seeing, they do not see; though hearing, they do not hear or understand.

In them is fulfilled the prophecy of Isaiah:

'You will be ever hearing but never understanding;

you will be ever seeing but never perceiving.

For this people's heart has become calloused;

they hardly hear with their ears,

and they have closed their eyes.

Otherwise they might see with their eyes,

hear with their ears

understand with their hearts

and turn, and I would heal them.'

But blessed are your eyes because they see, and your ears because they hear. For I tell you the truth, many prophets and righteous men longed to see what you see but did not see it, and to hear what you hear but did not hear it.

Listen then to what the parable of the sower means: When anyone hears the message about the kingdom and does not understand it, the evil one comes and snatches away what was sown in his heart. This is the seed sown along the path. The one who received the seed that fell on rocky places is the man who hears the word and at once receives it with joy. But since he has no root, he lasts only a short time. When trouble or persecution comes because of the word, he quickly falls away. The one who received the seed that fell among the thorns is the man who hears the word, but the worries of this life and the deceitfulness of wealth choke it, making it unfruitful. But the one who received the seed that fell on good soil is the man who hears the word and understands it. He produces a crop, yielding a hundred, sixty or thirty times what was sown."

Let us look at this passage in the light of the original context. Many heard the message that day as Jesus spoke. Many listened intently and heard every word. Yet as they left, some never heard what was said. When questioned about his choice of speaking in parables, Jesus quoted from Isaiah "though seeing, they do not see; though hearing, they do not hear or understand." He explained that many in the audience never really heard what he said, because they were listening with an attitude not to receive. There was nothing wrong with the seed, but even though it was sown much of the good seed would never produce a crop. It was wasted on hardened hearts.

Earlier in the chapter we quoted a passage from John 5 where Jesus spoke to the religious leaders of the day and said that they diligently studied the Scriptures, yet failed to recognize the fact that those very Scriptures reveal him as the Messiah. In fact, the most surprising aspect of the story of Jesus is how those who should have recognized him never did. The religious leaders, who knew the Scriptures better than most, were those who were most opposed to Jesus and rejected his message. In terms of the parable of the sower, the seed did not fall in the good soil and did not produce a crop.

In Hebrews 3-4 we find a similar message. Having first warned the readers in Hebrews 2:1 "we must pay careful attention to what we have heard," the author continued with a warning against unbelief in the next chapter. Having recalled the history of the people of Israel after the Exodus as example, he then said:

"Therefore, since the promise of entering his rest still stands, let us be careful that none of you be found to have fallen short of it. <u>For we also have had the gospel preached to us, just as they did; but the message they heard was of no value to them, because those who heard did not combine it with faith.</u>" Hebrews 4:1-2.

Ultimately the Word of God must be combined with faith to become fruitful. In Romans 9-11 Paul wrote about his sorrow that so many of his own people rejected the message of Jesus. In Romans 10:16-21 he writes:

But not all the Israelites accepted the good news. For Isaiah says, "Lord, who has believed our message?" <u>Consequently, faith comes from hearing the message,</u> and the message is *heard through the word of Christ. But I ask: Did they not hear? Of course, they did:*

> *"Their voice has gone out into all the earth, their words to the ends of the world."*

> *Again, I ask: Did Israel not understand? First, Moses says,*

> *"I will make you envious by those who are not a nation;*

> *I will make you angry by a nation that has no understanding."*

> *And Isaiah boldly says,*

> *"I was found by those who did not seek me;*

> *I revealed myself to those who did not ask for me."*

> *But concerning Israel he says,*

> *"All day long I have held out my hands*

> *to a disobedient and obstinate people."*

Note that faith comes by hearing. When we truly hear, it leads to faith. This is the foundation of the passage in James 2:14-26:

What good is it, my brothers, if a man claims to have faith but has no deeds? Can such faith save him? Suppose a brother or sister is without clothes and daily food. If one of you says to him, "Go, I wish you well; keep warm and well fed," but does nothing about his physical needs, what good is it? In the same way, faith by itself, if it is not accompanied by action, is dead.

But someone will say, "You have faith; I have deeds."

Show me your faith without deeds, and I will show you my faith by what I do. You believe that there is one God. Good! Even the demons believe that - and shudder.

You foolish man, do you want evidence that faith without deeds is useless? Was not our ancestor Abraham considered righteous for what he did when he offered his son Isaac on the altar? You see that his faith and his actions were working together, and his faith was made complete by what he did. And the scripture was fulfilled that says, "Abraham believed God, and it was credited to him as righteousness," and he was called God's friend. You see that a person is justified by what he does and not by faith alone.

In the same way, was not even Rahab the prostitute considered righteous for what she did when she gave lodging to the spies and sent them off in a different direction? As the body without the spirit is dead, so faith without deeds is dead.

Faith comes by hearing. When we truly hear the word of God it has to produce a radical and authentic faith within us. That faith will be visible in our lives as we walk with a radical authenticity that cannot be missed. This is illustrated in the fact that before the believers were called Christians, they were known as "followers of the Way!" We find many references to this in the Book of Acts — e.g.

Acts 9:2; 16:17; 19:9 and 23; 24:14 and 22, etc. This is the basis of the admonition in Hebrews 13:7-8:

Remember your leaders, who spoke the word of God to you. <u>Consider the outcome of their way of life and imitate their faith.</u> Jesus Christ is the same yesterday and today and forever.

Let us take a minute or two and look at these verses again. The word of God spoken forth and taught by the leaders is to be illustrated by their way of life, in order for the followers to imitate. With this in mind Paul urged the Corinthians to follow his example as we read in 1 Corinthians 4:14-17 and again in 1 Corinthians 11:1-2:

I am not writing this to shame you, but to warn you, as my dear children. Even though you have ten thousand guardians in Christ, you do not have many fathers, for in Christ Jesus I became your father through the gospel. <u>Therefore, I urge you to imitate me. For this reason, I am sending to you Timothy, my son whom I love, who is faithful in the Lord. He will remind you of my way of life in Christ Jesus, which agrees with what I teach</u> everywhere in every church.

<u>Follow my example, as I follow the example of Christ. I praise you for remembering me in everything and for holding to the teachings, just as I passed them on to you.</u>

The man called Jesus Christ first and foremost illustrated the way of life. He did not just speak forth the word of God with authority, but he lived it out in a radical and authentic way. Some, who met him and listened to his word, heard him and faith arose in them. Their lives were changed and they became known as followers of the Way, as they walked in a radical authenticity that set them apart from everyone else. Today this same Jesus is challenging those who call themselves his followers to this radical authenticity. This challenge is to listen to the Spirit and to hear his voice. Those who hear find that their eyes are opened in faith and they see as if for the first time: They see a vision of the Kingdom of heaven. Let us listen and see for ourselves!

A KINGDOM MINDSET

*I*t is a well-known fact that Jesus spoke very little about the church, but very much about the Kingdom of God or the Kingdom of heaven. **Did you hear that with me? It is not about the church it is about the Kingdom of God!** There is a major difference. The church is not the Kingdom. To have a vision for the church does not mean one has a Kingdom vision. So, what is this Kingdom all about? Let us begin by listening to Jesus as he spoke with Pilate as recorded in John 18:33-37:

Pilate then went back inside the palace, summoned Jesus and asked him, "Are you the king of the Jews?"

"Is that your own idea," Jesus asked, "or did others talk to you about me?"

"Am I a Jew?" Pilate replied. "It was your people and your chief priests who handed you over to me. What is it you have done?"

Jesus said, "My kingdom is not of this world. If it were, my servants would fight to prevent my arrest by the Jews. But now my kingdom is from another place."

"You are a king, then!" said Pilate.

Jesus answered, "You are right in saying I am a king. In fact, for this reason I was born, and for this I came into the world, to testify to the truth. Everyone on the side of truth listens to me."

This Kingdom is not of this world and it functions very differently from the worldly kingdoms. In the passage above Jesus referred to the fact that he did not allow his followers to resist his arrest by the Jews, for his Kingdom functions differently. That is why Jesus used the terms "Kingdom of God" and "Kingdom of heaven" to describe this Kingdom. It is not of this world and often will not make sense to the world, for God says in Isaiah 55:8-9:

"For my thoughts are not your thoughts,

neither are your ways my ways," declares the LORD.

"As the heavens are higher than the earth,

so are my ways higher than your ways

and my thoughts than your thoughts.

This is nowhere better illustrated than in the death of Jesus on the cross. That is why the apostle Paul wrote in 1 Corinthians 1:18-25:

For the message of the cross is foolishness to those who are perishing, but to us who are being saved it is the power of God. For it is written:

"I will destroy the wisdom of the wise;

the intelligence of the intelligent I will frustrate."

Where is the wise man? Where is the scholar? Where is the philosopher of this age? Has not God made foolish the wisdom of the world? For since in the wisdom of God the world through its wisdom did not know him, God was pleased through the foolishness of what was preached to save those who believe. Jews demand miraculous signs and Greeks look for wisdom, but we preach Christ crucified: a stumbling block to Jews and foolishness to Gentiles, but to those whom God has called, both Jews and Greeks, Christ the power of God and the wisdom of God. For the foolishness of God is wiser than man's wisdom, and the weakness of God is stronger than man's strength.

The Kingdom vision dawns in a human life when the truth of the cross is accepted. In accepting this message, one recognizes that God is the King and surrenders his/her life to him. The Kingdom is displayed in human lives lived in this submission to Jesus regardless of the cost. It calls for and births a radical authenticity in the way of life, lived in simple faith. The Kingdom vision is most clearly seen through the eyes of a child, for it calls for childlike faith. Listen how Jesus said it in Matthew 18:1-6:

At that time the disciples came to Jesus and asked, "Who is the greatest in the kingdom of heaven?"

He called a little child and had him stand among them. And he said: "I tell you the truth, unless you change and become like little children, you will never enter the kingdom of heaven. *Therefore, whoever humbles himself like this child is the greatest in the kingdom of heaven.*

"And whoever welcomes a little child like this in my name welcomes me. But if anyone causes one of these little ones who believe in me to sin, it would be better for him to have a large millstone hung around his neck and to be drowned in the depths of the sea."

Let us note this very clearly: Jesus literally said to his disciples that unless they change and become childlike, they would never enter into the Kingdom. The Kingdom vision can only be seen through childlike faith. This is far more than the tokenism of the church programs for children and youth in most churches. Listen again to a similar passage in Luke 18:15-17:

People were also bringing babies to Jesus to have him touch them. When the disciples saw this, they rebuked them. But Jesus called the children to him and said, "Let the little children come to me, and do not hinder them, for the kingdom of God belongs to such as these. I tell you the truth, anyone who will not receive the kingdom of God like a little child will never enter it."

In the tradition I was raised this passage was used to support the doctrine of infant baptism. Without going into that discussion, the truth is that the mothers were bringing their babies to receive a touch from Jesus. Matthew said they were brought so that Jesus could place his hands on them and pray for them (Matthew 19:13).

These little ones received a real touch from Jesus. Despite thousands of dollars being spent in North America on resources for Sunday school and Vacation Bible School, the vast majority of our children never meet Jesus in person. They leave church in their teen years without ever having encountered the risen Lord. **In terms of the words of Jesus in this passage, does the Sunday school programs help or hinder our children to develop a Kingdom vision?**

Let us explore this a little more. In the previous chapter we looked at Luke 10, which records the story of the seventy-two sent out by Jesus on a mission. They were to go in simple faith sharing the story of the Kingdom and demonstrating it by healing the sick. Then we read (Luke 10:17-21):

The seventy-two returned with joy and said, "Lord, even the demons submit to us in your name."

He replied, "I saw Satan fall like lightning from heaven. I have given you authority to trample on snakes and scorpions and to overcome all the power of the enemy; nothing will harm you. However, do not rejoice that the spirits submit to you, but rejoice that your names are written in heaven."

At that time Jesus, full of joy through the Holy Spirit, said, "I praise you, Father, Lord of heaven and earth, because you have hidden these things from the wise and learned, and revealed them to little children. Yes, Father, for this was your good pleasure."

Simple childlike faith produced miracles and the demonic forces had to submit. Even Satan was dislodged as they walked in simple faith. This is why Jesus prayed with joy saying that the Father has hidden these things from the wise and learned and revealed them to little children. This fact is very vividly illustrated in the history of Jesus' entry into Jerusalem on Palm Sunday as we read in Matthew 21:1-15:

As they approached Jerusalem and came to Bethphage on the Mount of Olives, Jesus sent two disciples, saying to them, "Go to the village ahead of you, and at once you will find a donkey tied there, with her colt by her. Untie them and bring them to me. If anyone says anything to you, tell him that the Lord needs them, and he will send them right away."

This took place to fulfill what was spoken through the prophet:

> *"Say to the Daughter of Zion, 'See, your*
> *king comes to you, gentle and riding on a*
> *donkey, on a colt, the foal of a donkey.'"*

The disciples went and did as Jesus had instructed them. They brought the donkey and the colt, placed their cloaks on them, and Jesus sat on them. A very large crowd spread their cloaks on the road, while others cut branches from the trees and spread them on the road. The crowds that went ahead of him and those that followed shouted,

> *"Hosanna to the Son of David!"*

> *"Blessed is he who comes in the name of the Lord!"*

> *"Hosanna in the highest!"*

When Jesus entered Jerusalem, the whole city was stirred and asked, "Who is this?" The crowds answered, "This is Jesus, the prophet from Nazareth in Galilee."

Jesus entered the temple area and drove out all who were buying and selling there. He overturned the tables of the money changers and the benches of those selling doves. "It is written," he said to them, "'My house will be called a house of prayer,' but you are making it a 'den of robbers.'"

The blind and the lame came to him at the temple, and he healed them. But when the chief priests and the teachers of the law saw the wonderful things he did and the children shouting in the temple area, "Hosanna to the Son of David," they were indignant.

"Do you hear what these children are saying?" they asked him.

"Yes," replied Jesus, "have you never read,

'From the lips of children and infants you have ordained praise'?"

On that day the learned and the wise failed to recognize the very one sent by the Father. The little ones saw God while the wise and learned missed the presence of the living God in their midst. In fact, they were offended by the celebration of the children. It is highly revealing that Jesus responded to their offense and question to him by quoting from Psalm 8. Let us read Psalm 8:1-2:

O LORD, our Lord,

how majestic is your name in all the earth!

You have set your glory

above the heavens.

From the lips of children and infants you have ordained praise

because of your enemies,

to silence the foe and the avenger.

Let us look at this in perspective: The praise of children and infants has been ordained by the Father to silence the enemies! The simple celebration of children shuts the mouth of the demonic forces! When Jesus stepped into the temple that day, he overturned the tables and cleansed the sanctuary. The leaders who had a vested interest in the status quo were indignant – but the children rejoiced. The little ones were able to see what the learned and wise missed and in the midst of this the enemy was dethroned as the Kingdom of God was revealed. The power of God broke through and blind and lame were healed.

Let us back up to another story which we touched on earlier, the mission of the seventy-two disciples. It is very important to note that we have no record of any names. In our terms today, they were ordinary people – no-names! They had no theological degrees and did not attend any major university of their day. They simply walked with a childlike faith and saw miracles as they shared the story of the Kingdom and laid hands on the sick. As Jesus said, "the Father revealed these things to the little ones, but hid them from the wise and the learned." **Could it be that the same is true in the church today? Could it be that with all our wisdom and knowledge manifested in our religious programs done in our magnificent buildings, we miss the very heart of the Father? Could it be that there is another and more effective way to serve God than the religious programs we follow in the buildings we call churches? Could it be that we can see the power of God and experience the presence of God without much of the current structures that we have taken for granted?**

Before we answer too quickly, let us take note of this: "Everyone should be quick to listen, but slow to speak." (James 1:19). Jesus said: *"But seek first his kingdom and his righteousness, and all these things will be given to you as well."* Matthew 6:33.

Within the context "all these things" refer to everything we devote most of our lives to have – needs like food and shelter. Jesus said we could have all of these met, provided we seek first the Kingdom of God and his righteousness. Let us therefore explore what this Kingdom vision is all about – for we need to see it to seek it!

SEEING WITH KINGDOM EYES

John 3:1-3:

Now there was a man of the Pharisees named Nicodemus, a member of the Jewish ruling council. He came to Jesus at night and said, "Rabbi, we know you are a teacher who has come from God. For no one could perform the miraculous signs you are doing if God were not with him."

In reply Jesus declared, "I tell you the truth, no one can see the kingdom of God unless he is born again."

To see through Kingdom eyes, that is to have a Kingdom vision, we need to be born again. Now within our culture the term "born again" is used and abused by many. We often hear that someone is a "born again" Christian or believer. For many this is their badge to separate them from "others" in the broader church. As we read the story of Nicodemus' meeting with Jesus, we note that what is at stake is the choice between two kingdoms. The issue is how to move from the kingdom of this world into the Kingdom of God. Nicodemus came in a very real sense seeking the Kingdom of God and Jesus said that the only way to enter into that Kingdom is to be born again. As the conversation continues Jesus explains that to be born again is to have a spiritual transformation.

John 3:4-21:

Jesus answered, "I tell you the truth, no one can enter the kingdom of God unless he is born of water and the Spirit. Flesh gives birth to flesh, but the Spirit gives birth to spirit. You should not be surprised at my saying, 'You must be born again.' The wind blows wherever it pleases. You hear its sound, but you cannot tell where it comes from or where it is going. So it is with everyone born of the Spirit."

"How can this be?" Nicodemus asked.

"You are Israel's teacher," said Jesus, "and do you not understand these things? I tell you the truth, we speak of what we know, and we testify to what we have seen, but still you people do not accept our testimony. I have spoken to you of earthly things and you do not believe; how then will you believe if I speak of heavenly things? No one has ever gone into heaven except the one who came from heaven - the Son of Man. Just as Moses lifted up the snake in the desert, so the Son of Man must be lifted up, that everyone who believes in him may have eternal life.

"For God so loved the world that he gave his one and only Son, that whoever believes in him shall not perish but have eternal life. For God did not send his Son into the world

to condemn the world, but to save the world through him. Whoever believes in him is not condemned, but whoever does not believe stands condemned already because he has not believed in the name of God's one and only Son. This is the verdict: Light has come into the world, but men loved darkness instead of light because their deeds were evil. Everyone who does evil hates the light, and will not come into the light for fear that his deeds will be exposed. But whoever lives by the truth comes into the light, so that it may be seen plainly that what he has done has been done through God."

The issue about our faith has nothing to do with "church membership" or some religious traditions. It has nothing to do with church buildings and programs run mostly on Sunday. It has nothing to do with leaders running around with titles like "pastor" or "the minister" or "reverent" or "the bishop". **It has everything to do with the Kingdom and a Kingdom lifestyle. Entering into that Kingdom lifestyle calls for a spiritual transformation rooted in the acceptance of the love of God revealed in the person of Jesus Christ. This spiritual transformation is an absolute necessity. We have to be born again to see this Kingdom. It calls for a radical transformation and enables us to look at all of life through the eyes of God. It begins when we truly recognize the radical love of God for the world. It is radical in every way. To enter into this Kingdom lifestyle a person has to make the radical decision to accept this love and implicit in this is the acceptance of the fact that it is only to be found through the man called Jesus. There is no other way!**

John 14:6:

Jesus answered, "I am the way and the truth and the life. No one comes to the Father except through me."

As the church was birthed, we find that this was the very basis of their faith. In Acts 4 there is a story of the apostles walking in this Kingdom way and being challenged after a miraculous healing in the temple and we read Acts 4:7-12:

They had Peter and John brought before them and began to question them: "By what power or what name did you do this?"

Then Peter, filled with the Holy Spirit, said to them: "Rulers and elders of the people! If we are being called to account today for an act of kindness shown to a cripple and are asked how he was healed, then know this, you and all the people of Israel: It is by the name of Jesus Christ of Nazareth, whom you crucified but whom God raised from the dead, that this man stands before you healed. He is

> *"'the stone you builders rejected,*
>
> *which has become the capstone.'*

<u>Salvation is found in no one else, for there is no other name under heaven given to men by which we must be saved."</u>

In our society the very idea of such an absolute claim is offensive and deemed to be unacceptable. Thus, many in the church (and many who call themselves "born again believers") are not willing to be that radical and state this as the starting point of their faith. **However, the way of life called forth by Jesus begins when through a spiritual transformation a person's eyes are opened to accept him and him alone as Lord and to submit to him in every way.**

Entering into the Kingdom calls for a radical transformation of life and can only happen through a spiritual birth in which a person is totally changed. It begins by seeing the man Jesus Christ through spiritual eyes and accepting him as Lord. It is as if a veil is removed from one's eyes, as we read in 2 Corinthians 3:16-18:

But whenever anyone turns to the Lord, the veil is taken away. Now the Lord is the Spirit, and where the Spirit of the Lord is, there is freedom. And we, who with unveiled faces all reflect the Lord's glory, are being transformed into his likeness with ever-increasing glory, which comes from the Lord, who is the Spirit.

This is extremely important! The key to our faith is to recognize the Holy Spirit as we look at the man called Jesus Christ. It is in the relationship with Jesus that we get to know the heart of God and see the glory of God revealed in him. It opens the door to true spirituality. In looking at Jesus this glory is reflected from us so that the world can see the glory of God. Our relationship with Jesus literally changes us so that we become more like him. The Greek word translated as "we are being transformed" is the word "metamorphoo" from which we derive the word "metamorphosis." In Christ we get a totally new nature. This same word is also found in Romans 12 which is also equally important to note. Romans 12:1-2 reads as follows:

Therefore, I urge you, brothers, in view of God's mercy, to offer your bodies as living sacrifices, holy and pleasing to God-this is your spiritual act of worship. <u>Do not conform any longer to the pattern of this world, but be transformed by the renewing of your mind</u>. Then you will be able to test and approve what God's will is-his good, pleasing and perfect will.

One of the things that happens when our eyes are opened and the veil removed is that we begin to see everything in a different light. Included in this is that our mindsets need to be changed and as we walk in relationship with Jesus they will be changed. Patterns of thinking and patterns of looking at things are transformed and as this happens it leads to a new way of life. This new way of life is all encompassing. There is no exception. There is not any little area or compartment that can be left unaffected. In fact, one of the very patterns that need to be changed relates to the understanding of what it is to have a Kingdom mindset. Let us illustrate this by looking at the preparation for the revelation of Jesus Christ through the preaching of John as recalled in Matthew 3:1-12:

In those days John the Baptist came, preaching in the Desert of Judea and saying, "Repent, <u>for the kingdom of heaven is near.</u>" This is he who was spoken of through the prophet Isaiah:

"A voice of one calling in the desert,

'Prepare the way for the Lord,

make straight paths for him.'"

John's clothes were made of camel's hair, and he had a leather belt around his waist. His food was locusts and wild honey. People went out to him from Jerusalem and all Judea and the whole region of the Jordan. Confessing their sins, they were baptized by him in the Jordan River.

But when he saw many of the Pharisees and Sadducees coming to where he was baptizing, he said to them: "You brood of vipers! Who warned you to flee from the coming wrath? <u>Produce fruit in keeping with repentance.</u> And do not think you can say to yourselves, 'We have Abraham as our father.' I tell you that out of these stones God can raise up children for Abraham. The ax is already at the root of the trees, and every tree that does not produce good fruit will be cut down and thrown into the fire.

<u>I baptize you with water for repentance. But after me will come one who is more powerful than I, whose sandals I am not fit to carry. He will baptize you with the Holy Spirit and with fire. His winnowing fork is in his hand, and he will clear his threshingfloor, gathering his wheat into the barn and burning up the chaff with unquenchable fire."</u>

The announcement of the coming Kingdom came with a call to repentance. John called the people of Israel to repent, as Jesus' ministry was about to usher in the

Kingdom. The Greek word for "repent" is "metanoia" which means to turn around and walk in the opposite direction. It implies a radical change in thinking and leads to a radically different way of action. In fact, as John saw the Pharisees and Sadducees coming to him, he had very strong words for them. However, the key issue was that John said that true repentance leads to lives that produce specific fruit in line with the changed mindset. **Putting these together, the proof of being born again is seen in a Kingdom lifestyle where the very glory of Jesus is reflected for the world to see.**

This lifestyle is radically different from the worldly concepts. It begins with the challenge to accept Jesus and his way as the only way to the Father. The only way to live this lifestyle is to keep focused on him and be prepared to pay the price of a radically committed life to be a follower of the man who gave all he had even to death on a cross. This does not come easily. Following a summary of the price paid by heroes of the faith in Hebrews 11, the author continued in Hebrews 12:1-14:

Therefore, since we are surrounded by such a great cloud of witnesses, let us throw off everything that hinders and the sin that so easily entangles, and let us run with perseverance the race marked out for us. Let us fix our eyes on Jesus, the author and perfecter of our faith, who for the joy set before him endured the cross, scorning its shame, and sat down at the right hand of the throne of God. Consider him who endured such opposition from sinful men, so that you will not grow weary and lose heart.

<u>In your struggle against sin, you have not yet resisted to the point of shedding your blood.</u> And you have forgotten that word of encouragement that addresses you as sons:

> *"My son, do not make light of the Lord's discipline, and do not lose heart when he rebukes you, because the Lord disciplines those he loves, and he punishes everyone he accepts as a son."*

Endure hardship as discipline; God is treating you as sons. For what son is not disciplined by his father? If you are not disciplined (and everyone undergoes discipline), then you are illegitimate children and not true sons. Moreover, we have all had human fathers who disciplined us and we respected them for it. How much more should we submit to the Father of our spirits and live! Our fathers disciplined us for a little while as they thought best; but God disciplines us for our good, that we may share in his holiness. No discipline seems pleasant at the time, but painful. Later on, however, it produces a harvest of righteousness and peace for those who have been trained by it.

Therefore, strengthen your feeble arms and weak knees. "Make level paths for your feet," so that the lame may not be disabled, but rather healed.

Make every effort to live in peace with all men and to be holy; without holiness no one will see the Lord.

This lifestyle calls for radical obedience and commitment. The Kingdom vision is not for those who want easy answers. It calls for a willingness to reject and throw away everything that will hinder the image of Jesus to show forth in one's life. He is the author and finisher of our faith and his life is the very essence of what it means to walk in the Way and to be authentic. The cross is not a cute piece of jewelry to wear or a symbol on the wall in a building called a church. It calls for a death of the ways of the world and showing forth faith in a radical authentic lifestyle. Make no mistake, this lifestyle is radical and there is no way around it. It challenges the very human worldly patterns of thinking and more than often turns "conventional thinking" upside down. This is very pointedly illustrated in Jesus' sermon on the mount, e.g. the opening words we call the beatitudes. Just read these with me and listen to the implication of the words, Matthew 5:3-12:

"Blessed are the poor in spirit,

for theirs is the kingdom of heaven.

Blessed are those who mourn,

for they will be comforted.

Blessed are the meek,

for they will inherit the earth.

Blessed are those who hunger and thirst for righteousness,

for they will be filled.

Blessed are the merciful,

for they will be shown mercy.

Blessed are the pure in heart,

for they will see God.

Blessed are the peacemakers,

for they will be called sons of God.

<u>*Blessed are those who are persecuted because of righteousness, for theirs is the kingdom of heaven.*</u>

Blessed are you when people insult you, persecute you and falsely say all kinds of evil against you because of me. Rejoice and be glad, because great is your reward in heaven, for in the same way they persecuted the prophets who were before you."

Without going into any detail, note who are promised the Kingdom of heaven! Also, just try to sell the idea of the meek inheriting the earth to Wall Street – or to the Church Board for that matter! However, Jesus did not speak these words to be empty promises or just ideas to ponder. These words, which turn conventional wisdom upside down, set the stage for the Kingdom way of life bringing light into the darkness of the world so that those in the dark can see the presence of the Father as we read in Matthew 5:13-16:

"You are the salt of the earth. But if the salt loses its saltiness, how can it be made salty again? It is no longer good for anything, except to be thrown out and trampled by men.

You are the light of the world. A city on a hill cannot be hidden. Neither do people light a lamp and put it under a bowl. Instead they put it on its stand, and it gives light to everyone in the house. In the same way, let your light shine before men, that they may see your good deeds and praise your Father in heaven."

Let us not miss the very obvious! The spiritual transformation that enables us to recognize the radical love of the Father in Jesus Christ calls forth faith that shows itself in lives lived with a radical authenticity. The grace we freely received in Jesus Christ is not cheap. He did not die on the cross just to hand out free tickets to eternity! He suffered and gave his life to enable us to enter into the Kingdom and walk in the Way of the Kingdom as he did even here on earth. In much of the evangelical mindsets grace has become very cheap and we pride ourselves that we do not live under the law – yet Jesus was very explicit that the Way of the Kingdom is even more radical than expected! Matthew 5:17-20:

Do not think that I have come to abolish the Law or the Prophets; I have not come to abolish them but to fulfill them. I tell you the truth, until heaven and earth disappear, not the smallest letter, not the least stroke of a pen, will by any means disappear from the Law until everything is accomplished. Anyone who breaks one of the least of these commandments and teaches others to do the same will be called least in the kingdom of heaven, but whoever practices and teaches these commands will be called great in the kingdom of heaven. <u>For I tell you that unless your righteousness surpasses that of the Pharisees and the teachers of the law, you will certainly not enter the kingdom of heaven.</u>

Following these words, we find Jesus outlining specific details regarding this Way of life and the Kingdom lifestyle. In the pages to follow we will focus on some of these in more detail, but for the moment it is important to get an overview. Thus, let us listen to the conclusion of the Sermon on the Mount in Matthew 7:15-27:

"Watch out for false prophets. They come to you in sheep's clothing, but inwardly they are ferocious wolves. <u>By their fruit you will recognize them. Do people pick grapes from thorn bushes, or figs from thistles? Likewise, every good tree bears good fruit, but a bad tree bears bad fruit. A good tree cannot bear bad fruit, and a bad tree cannot bear good fruit. Every tree that does not bear good fruit is cut down and thrown into the fire. Thus, by their fruit you will recognize them.</u>

<u>Not everyone who says to me, 'Lord, Lord,' will enter the kingdom of heaven, but only he who does the will of my Father who is in heaven.</u> Many will say to me on that day, 'Lord, Lord, did we not prophesy in your name, and in your name drive out demons and perform many miracles?' Then I will tell them plainly, 'I never knew you. Away from me, you evildoers!'

<u>Therefore, everyone who hears these words of mine and puts them into practice is like a wise man who built his house on the rock.</u> The rain came down, the streams rose, and the winds blew and beat against that house; yet it did not fall, because it had its foundation on the rock. But everyone who hears these words of mine and does not put them into practice is like a foolish man who built his house on sand. The rain

came down, the streams rose, and the winds blew and beat against that house, and it fell with a great crash."

In a real sense we again face the truth that faith comes by hearing! When we hear the words of the Lord faith arises and that faith leads to a spiritually productive lifestyle. It is the Kingdom Way of life that brings forth fruit. Do not miss the fact that the words of Jesus to be put into practice in the context are the very radical words recorded in the Sermon on the Mount. **In plain words: Unless our faith is authentic and visibly demonstrated in this radical lifestyle bringing fruit that cannot be missed, we will not enter the Kingdom.**

Let us now turn our vision to see the way to a fruitful life.

A FRUITFUL VINE

John 15:1-17

"I am the true vine, and my Father is the gardener. He cuts off every branch in me that bears no fruit, while every branch that does bear fruit, he prunes so that it will be even more fruitful. You are already clean because of the word I have spoken to you. _Remain in me, and I will remain in you._ No branch can bear fruit by itself; it must remain in the vine. Neither can you bear fruit unless you _remain in me._

I am the vine; you are the branches. If a man _remains in me_ and I in him, he will bear much fruit; apart from me you can do nothing. If anyone does _not remain in me_, he is like a branch that is thrown away and withers; such branches are picked up, thrown into the fire and burned. If you _remain in me_ and my words remain in you, ask whatever you wish, and it will be given you. _This is to my Father's glory, that you bear much fruit, showing yourselves to be my disciples._

As the Father has loved me, so have I loved you. _Now remain in my love. If you obey my commands, you will remain in_ *my love, just as I have obeyed my Father's commands and remain in his love. I have told you this so that my joy may be in you and that your joy may be complete. My command is this: Love each other as I have loved you. Greater love has no one than this, that he lay down his life for his friends. You are my friends if you do what I command. I no longer call you servants, because a servant does not know his master's business. Instead, I have called you friends, for everything that I learned from my Father I have made known to you. You did not choose me, but I chose you and appointed you to go and bear fruit - fruit that will last. Then the Father will give you whatever you ask in my name. This is my command: Love each other."*

These well-known words of Jesus need no explanation. The key to a fruitful Kingdom life is to be intimately connected with the man Jesus Christ. Over and over he said that the fruit comes forth as we are connected with him and remain in him. **This intimate relationship with Jesus is the key to release the productive Kingdom life that brings glory to the Father!** Note that it is in the fruit that the glory of God is revealed.

With that let us take a step back in time to the prophetic word of Habakkuk 2. This chapter opens with these words: Habakkuk 2:1-3:

> *I will stand at my watch*
>
> *and station myself on the ramparts;*
>
> *I will look to see what he will say to me,*
>
> *and what answer I am to give to this complaint.*

Then the LORD replied:

> *"Write down the revelation*
>
> *and make it plain on tablets*
>
> *so that a herald may run with it.*
>
> *For the revelation awaits an appointed time;*
>
> *it speaks of the end*
>
> *and will not prove false.*
>
> *Though it lingers, wait for it;*
>
> *it will certainly come and will not delay."*

Following these words there is a revelation of a world in turmoil with corruption and violence. However, in the midst of these pictures we find the prophetic word of Habakkuk 2:14:

For the earth will be filled with the knowledge of the glory of the LORD, as the waters cover the sea.

The prophetic vision is a clear and plain revelation for the appointed time. It is sure to come. It involves the breaking forth of the Kingdom of God in the midst of a world in turmoil and unrighteousness. As the waters cover the sea, so shall the knowledge of the glory of the Lord fill the earth. The word here translated as "knowledge" literally means that which is ascertained by seeing. Thus, the prophetic word declares that there is a day coming when the glory of the Lord will be seen and will be able to be seen over the whole earth. This is nothing else than the Kingdom of God being made manifest in the earth. This is what Jesus meant when he spoke about us being the salt of the earth and the light of the world. It is in living this radical and authentic Kingdom lifestyle that the glory of God becomes visible to the world. It is a way of life that defies the logic and mindset of the world. It is rooted in the love of God made visible in Christ and receives its sustaining power from the relationship with Jesus. In and through this relationship that same love is made manifest in our lives as we live as citizens of this Kingdom.

This is not an easy way of life. It calls for sacrifice and a willingness to love unconditionally. It is rooted in the love of God in Jesus that was most visibly illustrated on the cross! In the passage about the vine and the branches Jesus spoke about the fruit that comes as we are connected with him and drew the attention to the fact that the fruit is the result of the love being made manifest in us and in the way we treat one another. Then he continued to spell out the price to be paid for this way of life in John 15:18-16:4:

If the world hates you, keep in mind that it hated me first. If you belonged to the world, it would love you as its own. As it is, you do not belong to the world, but I have chosen you out of the world. That is why the world hates you. Remember the words I spoke to you: 'No servant is greater than his master.' If they persecuted me, they will persecute you also. If they obeyed my teaching, they will obey yours also. They will treat you this way because of my name, for they do not know the One who sent me. If I had not come and spoken to them, they would not be guilty of sin. Now, however, they have no excuse for their sin. He who hates me hates my Father as well. If I had not done among them what no one else did, they would not be guilty of sin. But now they have seen these miracles, and yet they have hated both me and my Father. But this is to fulfill what is written in their Law: 'They hated me without reason.'

When the Counselor comes, whom I will send to you from the Father, the Spirit of truth who goes out from the Father, he will testify about me. And you also must testify, for you have been with me from the beginning.

All this I have told you so that you will not go astray. They will put you out of the synagogue; in fact, a time is coming when anyone who kills you will think he is offering a service to God. They will do such things because they have not known the Father or me. I have told you this, so that when the time comes you will remember that I warned you. I did not tell you this at first because I was with you.

Let us connect some of the dots. The revelation of the glory of the Lord comes through the lives of people who are willing to let the love of Christ transform them to the point of being willing to undergo suffering and persecution for the sake of pursuing the way of the Kingdom. The glory is made visible in and through lives displaying the love of God revealed in Christ. It is a love that enables us to see others through the eyes of God's incredible love displayed in Jesus. Where that love is expressed the Kingdom of God is seen and the glory of God revealed. It is in and through this that lives are touched and transformed which is nothing else but the manifestation of the fruit of the Spirit.

Let us look at this again and as we do this, listen to the voice of the Spirit. As we read through the stories in the Gospels, where do we find Jesus most often and what did he do? The answer is simple: He is found in different places in the community and wherever he is, he touches lives. He sees what many others miss. He looks through Kingdom tinted glasses as no other person and imparts life and hope and direction and much more. As Luke tells the story of the Good News revealed in Jesus, the beginning of his ministry is recorded in Chapter 4. Following his baptism and temptation he returned to Galilee in the power of the Spirit. As he taught in the synagogues his name became known in the region. Then he visited his hometown and, on the Sabbath, read from the scroll of the prophet Isaiah, recorded in Luke 4:18-19:

> *"The Spirit of the Lord is on me,*
>
> *because he has anointed me*
>
> *to preach good news to the poor.*
>
> *He has sent me to proclaim freedom for the prisoners*
>
> *and recovery of sight for the blind,*
>
> *to release the oppressed,*
>
> *to proclaim the year of the Lord's favor."*

Rolling up the scroll he publicly declared that these prophetic words were to be the basis of his ministry or to put it in other words, these words are foundational to the Kingdom of God for which he entered into this world and for which he would give his life on the cross. Then we read Luke 4:22-30:

All spoke well of him and were amazed at the gracious words that came from his lips.

"Isn't this Joseph's son?" they asked.

Jesus said to them, "Surely you will quote this proverb to me: 'Physician, heal yourself!

Do here in your hometown what we have heard that you did in Capernaum.'"

"I tell you the truth," he continued, "no prophet is accepted in his hometown. I assure you that there were many widows in Israel in Elijah's time, when the sky was shut for three and a half years and there was a severe famine throughout the land. Yet Elijah was not sent to any of them, but to a widow in Zarephath in the region of Sidon. And there were many in Israel with leprosy in the time of Elisha the prophet, yet not one of them was cleansed - only Naaman the Syrian."

All the people in the synagogue were furious when they heard this. They got up, drove him out of the town, and took him to the brow of the hill on which the town was built, in order to throw him down the cliff. But he walked right through the crowd and went on his way.

It is very interesting to read how Matthew recorded the same story, Matthew 13:54-58:

Coming to his hometown, he began teaching the people in their synagogue, and they were amazed. "Where did this man get this wisdom and these miraculous powers?" they asked. "Isn't this the carpenter's son? Isn't his mother's name Mary, and aren't his brothers James, Joseph, Simon and Judas? Aren't all his sisters with us? Where then did this man get all these things?" And they took offense at him.

But Jesus said to them, "Only in his hometown and in his own house is a prophet without honor."

<u>And he did not do many miracles there because of their lack of faith.</u>

Without going into a detailed discussion, let us note some things about this story. Jesus' ministry was less effective in his hometown, because the people took offense at his words. They could not see past the person they saw growing up and wanted to limit him to their expectations of faith. They heard the same words many others heard, but were not receptive and the words fell on the hard soil and it did not bring forth faith. They were offended because he walked in an anointing of the Spirit that they did not have and thus they rejected him. The same happened a few years later as his followers, having been filled with the Spirit on the day of Pentecost, walked in power and an anointing that astounded the wise and the learned as we read in Acts 4 following the miraculous healing of a crippled man, Acts 4:13-20:

When they saw the courage of Peter and John and realized that they were unschooled, ordinary men, they were astonished and they took note that these men had been with Jesus. But since they could see the man who had been healed standing there with them, there was nothing they could say. So, they ordered them to withdraw from the Sanhedrin and then conferred together. "What are we going to do with these men?" they asked. "Everybody living in Jerusalem knows they have done an outstanding miracle, and we cannot deny it. But to stop this thing from spreading any further among the people, we must warn these men to speak no longer to anyone in this name."

Then they called them in again and commanded them not to speak or teach at all in the name of Jesus. But Peter and John replied, "Judge for yourselves whether it is right in God's sight to obey you rather than God. For we cannot help speaking about what we have seen and heard."

Before we continue to look at the story of Jesus, we must note the obvious. The Kingdom of God often comes through the most unlikely vessels. In the eyes of the people of Nazareth, the little kid that grew up in the house of Joe and Mary and played ball in the street with their kids could never have been the Messiah. To the Pharisees and Teachers of the law, the unschooled and untrained fishermen from Galilee should not be able or allowed to teach and heal people. Today the same offense and rejection is growing as the Third Day Church arises and the No-names begin to walk in an anointing and authority that is lacking in the Church,

as we have known it in our society. Growing numbers meeting in homes without trained and ordained clergy minister in a greater power and anointing than most who spent years at the approved schools to get the credentials required for "the Ministry." There is a new reformation underway that will shatter the current structures as much as the Good News (gospel) of the Kingdom of God in Jesus Christ shattered the wineskin of Judaism in the first century.

For now, let us return to the foundations of the Kingdom as Jesus laid them out in the Synagogue in Nazareth and see how these prophetic words were fulfilled in him by looking at a few examples:

Directly following the incident in Nazareth, we read Luke 4:31-44:

Then he went down to Capernaum, a town in Galilee, and on the Sabbath began to teach the people. They were amazed at his teaching, because his message had authority.

In the synagogue there was a man possessed by a demon, an evil spirit. He cried out at the top of his voice, "Ha! What do you want with us, Jesus of Nazareth? Have you come to destroy us? I know who you are - the Holy One of God!"

"Be quiet!" Jesus said sternly. "Come out of him!" Then the demon threw the man down before them all and came out without injuring him.

All the people were amazed and said to each other, "What is this teaching? With authority and power, he gives orders to evil spirits and they come out!" And the news about him spread throughout the surrounding area.

Jesus left the synagogue and went to the home of Simon. Now Simon's mother-in-law was suffering from a high fever, and they asked Jesus to help her. So, he bent over her and rebuked the fever, and it left her. She got up at once and began to wait on them.

When the sun was setting, the people brought to Jesus all who had various kinds of sickness, and laying his hands on each one, he healed them. Moreover, demons came out of many people, shouting, "You are the Son of God!" But he rebuked them and would not allow them to speak, because they knew he was the Christ.

At daybreak Jesus went out to a solitary place. The people were looking for him and when they came to where he was, they tried to keep him from leaving them. But he said, "I must preach the good news of the kingdom of God to the other towns also, because that is why I was sent." And he kept on preaching in the synagogues of Judea.

As this example illustrates, the ministry of Jesus was marked by miraculous healings and setting people free from demonic oppression. Captives were released and the sick were healed. The ministry took place within and outside of the synagogues. **The hallmark of this ministry was that where there was a need, Jesus met the need when and where he encountered the need. It**

did not matter whether it was on the Sabbath or not, whether it was in the synagogue or not or whether it was approved by the religious establishment or not.

Further, he was sent to preach the good news of the Kingdom and this preaching was confirmed by the love of God made visible in power through miracles as the oppressed were set free, captives released and the sick healed. As Peter preached to the crowd on the day of Pentecost, he recalled the story of Jesus in these simple words in Acts 2:22-24:

Men of Israel, listen to this: <u>Jesus of Nazareth was a man accredited by God to you by miracles, wonders and signs, which God did among you through him, as you yourselves know.</u> This man was handed over to you by God's set purpose and foreknowledge; and you, with the help of wicked men, put him to death by nailing him to the cross. But God raised him from the dead, freeing him from the agony of death, because it was impossible for death to keep its hold on him.

Later when speaking to the Gentiles at the house of Cornelius we hear Peter's testimony summarizing the ministry of Jesus in the words recorded in Acts 10:34-46:

Then Peter began to speak: "I now realize how true it is that God does not show favoritism but accepts men from every nation who fear him and do what is right. You know the message God sent to the people of Israel, telling the good news of peace through Jesus Christ, who is Lord of all. <u>You know what has happened throughout Judea, beginning in Galilee after the baptism that John preached - how God anointed</u>

<u>Jesus of Nazareth with the Holy Spirit and power, and how he went around doing good and healing all who were under the power of the devil, because God was with him.</u>

We are witnesses of everything he did in the country of the Jews and in Jerusalem. They killed him by hanging him on a tree, but God raised him from the dead on the third day and caused him to be seen. He was not seen by all the people, but by witnesses whom God had already chosen - by us who ate and drank with him after he rose from the dead. He commanded us to preach to the people and to testify that he is the one whom God appointed as judge of the living and the dead. All the prophets testify about him that everyone who believes in him receives forgiveness of sins through his name."

While Peter was still speaking these words, the Holy Spirit came on all who heard the message. The circumcised believers who had come with Peter were astonished that the gift of the Holy Spirit had been poured out even on the Gentiles. For they heard them speaking in tongues and praising God.

The ministry of Jesus was marked by the proclamation of the good News about the Kingdom of God demonstrated in miracles as he met the needs of people wherever he went. As we read the stories recorded in the gospels, we find this on every page. He had the ability to see needs, which many missed. He saw the loneliness and rejection in the person of Zacchaeus, as he climbed a tree to see Jesus passing by in the midst of a crowd. He saw the brokenness of a lonely woman at the well, when all were taking their siesta. He saw the hurt and pain of the woman caught in adultery and condemned to be stoned to death by the religious hypocrites. He heard the cry of the Syro Phoenician woman, as she cried out to him to heal her child. He stopped on the way to a dying child to restore the life of a sick woman touching his clothes. **He saw these things because he was sent to demonstrate the love of God for this world, even unto death. Matthew shared the secret of his ministry in Matthew 9:35-38:**

Jesus went through all the towns and villages, teaching in their synagogues, preaching the good news of the kingdom and healing every disease and sickness. <u>When he saw the crowds, he had compassion on them, because they were harassed and helpless, like sheep without a shepherd.</u> Then he said to his disciples, "The harvest is plentiful but the workers are few. Ask the Lord of the harvest, therefore, to send out workers into his harvest field."

During his ministry on earth Jesus demonstrated the love of God in action. As he did this, he also trained his disciples to do the same. He spoke about these things over and over telling stories to illustrate the way of Kingdom living and what a Kingdom vision is all about. He shared stories about the shepherd leaving the ninety nine in the safety of the fold and seeking the single lost sheep; about the woman loosing a coin and sweeping the house to find it; about a younger son who walked away in arrogant rebellion and lost the whole inheritance to return in brokenness and repentance to the father and of the older brother who became jealous and angry as the father rejoiced when the younger one returned. In these and other stories he challenged the religious mindsets of the Jewish elite. He challenged the rich young man to invest his resources in full in the needs of the poor and to learn how to live the Kingdom life by looking through compassionate eyes to the needs of others. He challenged Simon the Pharisee to see the broken prostitute crying at the feet of Jesus, doing the very thing that he as host neglected to do when he did not wash Jesus' feet as the custom required. He preached a simple message of the Kingdom of God demonstrated in a lifestyle of radical authentic love with no boundaries and he expected his followers to do follow his example.

As he walked this earth, he spent time with a small group of disciples, training them and releasing them into the ministry. First, he sent out the twelve as we read in Luke 9:1-7:

When Jesus had called the Twelve together, he gave them power and authority to drive out all demons and to cure diseases, and he sent them out to preach the kingdom of God and to heal the sick. He told them: "Take nothing for the journey - no staff, no bag, no bread, no money, no extra tunic. Whatever house you enter, stay there until you leave that town. If people do not welcome you, shake the dust off your feet when you leave their town, as a testimony against them." So, they set out and went from village to village, preaching the gospel and healing people everywhere.

When they successfully completed the mission, he sent out seventy-two others in a similar way to do this ministry and then we read in Luke 11:17-20 how they successfully completed the mission:

The seventy-two returned with joy and said, "Lord, even the demons submit to us in your name."

He replied, "I saw Satan fall like lightning from heaven. I have given you authority to trample on snakes and scorpions and to overcome all the power of the enemy; nothing will harm you. However, do not rejoice that the spirits submit to you, but rejoice that your names are written in heaven."

At that time Jesus, full of joy through the Holy Spirit, said, "I praise you, Father, Lord of heaven and earth, because you have hidden these things from the wise and learned, and revealed them to little children. Yes, Father, for this was your good pleasure.

All things have been committed to me by my Father. No one knows who the Son is except the Father, and no one knows who the Father is except the Son and those to whom the Son chooses to reveal him."

Then he turned to his disciples and said privately, "Blessed are the eyes that see what you see. For I tell you that many prophets and kings wanted to see what you see but did not see it, and to hear what you hear but did not hear it."

When he spent his last night before his death on the cross with his closest friends, he spoke the words we noted above about the vine and the branches, in which he again made it clear that the Kingdom lifestyle is one of radical authentic love bringing forth fruit. At the end of this he released all of this to the Father in the prayer recorded in John 17. Let us simply read this prayer as it is with no commentary but allow the Spirit to speak to us:

After Jesus said this, he looked toward heaven and prayed

"Father, the time has come. Glorify your Son, that your Son may glorify you. For you granted him authority over all people that he might give eternal life to all those you have given him. Now this is eternal life: that they may know you, the only true God, and Jesus Christ, whom you have sent. <u>I have brought you glory on earth by completing the work you gave me to do.</u> And now, Father, glorify me in your presence with the glory I had with you before the world began.

<u>I have revealed you to those whom you gave me out of the world. They were yours; you gave them to me and they have obeyed your word. Now they know that everything you have given me comes from you. For I gave them the words you gave me and they accepted them.</u> They knew with certainty that I came from you, and they believed that you sent me. I pray for them. I am not praying for the world, but for those you have given me, for they are yours. All I have is yours, and all you have is mine. And glory has come to me through them. I will remain in the world no longer, but they are still in the world, and I am coming to you. Holy Father, protect them by the power of your name - the name you gave me - so that they may be one as we are one. While I was with them, I protected them and kept them safe by that name you gave me. None has been lost except the one doomed to destruction so that Scripture would be fulfilled. I am coming to you now, but I say these things while I am still in the world, so that they may have the full measure of my joy within them. I have

given them your word and the world has hated them, for they are not of the world any more than I am of the world. My prayer is not that you take them out of the world but that you protect them from the evil one. They are not of the world, even as I am not of it. Sanctify them by the truth; your word is truth. <u>As you sent me into the world, I have sent them into the world.</u> For them I sanctify myself, that they too may be truly sanctified.

<u>*My prayer is not for them alone. I pray also for those who will believe in me through their message, that all of them may be one, Father, just as you are in me and I am in you. May they also be in us so that the world may believe that you have sent me.*</u> *I have given them the glory that you gave me, that they may be one as we are one: I in them and you in me. May they be brought to complete unity to let the world know that you sent me and have loved them even as you have loved me.*

Father, I want those you have given me to be with me where I am, and to see my glory, the glory you have given me because you loved me before the creation of the world. Righteous Father, though the world does not know you, I know you, and they know that you have sent me. <u>I have made you known to them, and will continue to make you known in order that the love you have for me may be in them and that I myself may be in them.</u>"

Following his death and resurrection, the risen Lord again spoke forth the same message, e. g. John 20:19-23:

On the evening of that first day of the week, when the disciples were together, with the doors locked for fear of the Jews, Jesus

*came and stood among them and said, "Peace be with you!"
After he said this, he showed them his hands and side. The
disciples were overjoyed when they saw the Lord.*

*Again, Jesus said, "Peace be with you! <u>As the Father has sent
me, I am sending you.</u>" And with that he breathed on them
and said, "Receive the Holy Spirit. If you forgive anyone his
sins, they are forgiven; if you do not forgive them, they are
not forgiven."*

The same message is found in the Book of Acts where
Luke followed the recording of the gospel with the story of
how the kingdom vision led to the spread of the message
of the Kingdom through the early believers and the way
of life that made such an impact. The opening verses are
very important to get the picture, as we read Acts 1:1-8:

*In my former book, Theophilus, I wrote about all that Jesus
began to do and to teach until the day he was taken up to
heaven, after giving instructions through the Holy Spirit to
the apostles he had chosen. <u>After his suffering, he showed
himself to these men and gave many convincing proofs that
he was alive. He appeared to them over a period of forty days
and spoke about the kingdom of God.</u> On one occasion, while
he was eating with them, he gave them this command: "Do
not leave Jerusalem, but wait for the gift my Father promised,
which you have heard me speak about. For John baptized
with water, but in a few days, you will be baptized with the
Holy Spirit."*

*So, when they met together, they asked him, "Lord, are you
at this time going to restore the kingdom to Israel?"*

He said to them: "It is not for you to know the times or dates the Father has set by his own authority. But you will receive power when the Holy Spirit comes on you; and you will be my witnesses in Jerusalem, and in all Judea and Samaria, and to the ends of the earth."

In fact, the Book of Acts is very concisely summarized in the last two verses of the gospel according to Mark, Mark 16:19-20 which reads:

<u>After the Lord Jesus had spoken to them, he was taken up into heaven and he sat at the right hand of God. Then the disciples went out and preached everywhere, and the Lord worked with them and confirmed his word by the signs that accompanied it.</u>

Please note: Jesus came to preach and demonstrate the message of the Kingdom of God. Everything about Jesus has to do with the Kingdom. He opened the door to the Kingdom and challenged his followers to enter into a Kingdom lifestyle. This lifestyle has nothing to do with buildings and programs and steeples and traditions. It has everything to do with an intimate relationship with the Father and a willingness to walk in radical authenticity demonstrating the love of the Father that we received in and through the person of Jesus Christ. It is this love that compels us to live this radical lifestyle and to look at all of life and at people through God's eyes. This is the Kingdom vision, which leads to the radical lifestyle first witnessed in the person of Jesus Christ. Let us explore that now.

COMPELLING LOVE
IN ACTION

Nearly 2000 years ago on the way to Damascus to persecute those who followed what was known as "The Way", a man by the name of Saul of Tarsus met the risen Lord and as a result his life was changed forever. In the dust of the road, blinded and struck down, he encountered the transforming love of God in Christ and from that day on he was on a mission to preach the story and share this love. Years later in the second letter to the church in Corinth he wrote, 2 Corinthians 5:14-6:1:

For Christ's love compels us, because we are convinced that one died for all, and therefore all died. And he died for all, that those who live should no longer live for themselves but for him who died for them and was raised again.

So from now on we regard no one from a worldly point of view. Though we once regarded Christ in this way, we do so no longer. Therefore, if anyone is in Christ, he is a new creation; the old has gone, the new has come! All this is from God, who reconciled us to himself through Christ and gave us the ministry of reconciliation: that God was reconciling the world to himself in Christ, not counting men's sins against them. And he has committed to us the message of reconciliation. We are therefore Christ's ambassadors, as though God were making his appeal through us. We implore you on Christ's behalf: Be reconciled to God. God made him who had no sin to be sin for us, so that in him we might become the righteousness of God.

Those who encounter the love of God in Christ are changed and the way they view the world and especially people is changed forever. As we come to know Jesus, we are changed and we look at people through the lens of compassion. Those who learn to look at others through this lens move with compassion as Jesus did. In the process they come to see Jesus like they have never seen him before, as we read in Matthew 25:31-26:1:

"When the Son of Man comes in his glory, and all the angels with him, he will sit on his throne in heavenly glory. All the nations will be gathered before him, and he will separate the people one from another as a shepherd separates the sheep from the goats. He will put the sheep on his right and the goats on his left.

"Then the King will say to those on his right, 'Come, you who are blessed by my Father; take your inheritance, the kingdom prepared for you since the creation of the world. For I was hungry and you gave me something to eat, I was thirsty and you gave me something to drink, I was a stranger and you invited me in, I needed clothes and you clothed me, I was

sick and you looked after me, I was in prison and you came to visit me.'

"Then the righteous will answer him, 'Lord, when did we see you hungry and feed you, or thirsty and give you something to drink? When did we see you a stranger and invite you in, or needing clothes and clothe you? When did we see you sick or in prison and go to visit you?'

"<u>The King will reply, 'I tell you the truth, whatever you did for one of the least of these brothers of mine, you did for me.'</u>

"Then he will say to those on his left, 'Depart from me, you who are cursed, into the eternal fire prepared for the devil and his angels. For I was hungry and you gave me nothing to eat, I was thirsty and you gave me nothing to drink, I was a stranger and you did not invite me in, I needed clothes and you did not clothe me, I was sick and in prison and you did not look after me.'

"They also will answer, 'Lord, when did we see you hungry or thirsty or a stranger or needing clothes or sick or in prison, and did not help you?'

"He will reply, 'I tell you the truth, whatever you did not do for one of the least of these, you did not do for me.'

Then they will go away to eternal punishment, but the righteous to eternal life."

Let us cut through to the core here. This is not difficult to understand. The Kingdom vision is to be compelled

by the love of God to the point of responding to the needs of people as we encounter these needs. In this encounter we meet the risen Lord coming to us in the person in need. Our response indicates our willingness to live the Kingdom lifestyle and to walk in "The Way."

The well-known parable of the Good Samaritan is an excellent illustration of the point. The story began with an expert of the law asking Jesus what he could do to inherit eternal life. Then we read Luke 10:26-37:

"What is written in the Law?" Jesus replied. "How do you read it?"

He answered: <u>"Love the Lord your God with all your heart and with all your soul and with all your strength and with all your mind'; and, 'Love your neighbor as yourself.'" "You have answered correctly," Jesus replied. "Do this and you will live."</u>

But he wanted to justify himself, so he asked Jesus, "And who is my neighbor?"

In reply Jesus said: "A man was going down from Jerusalem to Jericho, when he fell into the hands of robbers. They stripped him of his clothes, beat him and went away, leaving him half dead. A priest happened to be going down the same road, and when he saw the man, he passed by on the other side. So too, a Levite, when he came to the place and saw him, passed by on the other side. But a Samaritan, as he traveled, came where the man was; and when he saw him, he took pity on him. He went to him and bandaged his wounds, pouring on oil and wine. Then he put the man on his own donkey, took him to an inn and took care of him. The next day he took out two silver coins and gave them to the innkeeper. 'Look after him,' he said, 'and when I return, I will reimburse you for any extra expense you may have.'

"Which of these three do you think was a neighbor to the man who fell into the hands of robbers?"

The expert in the law replied, "The one who had mercy on him." Jesus told him, "Go and do likewise."

Let us again note the obvious: Faith needs to be expressed in action or it is no faith at all. Without the visible expression of love by responding to the needs of others as we encounter these needs, we are simply religious unbelievers! This is what James expressed so pointedly in James 2:14-26:

What good is it, my brothers, if a man claims to have faith but has no deeds? Can such faith save him? Suppose a brother or sister is without clothes and daily food. If one of you says to him, "Go, I wish you well; keep warm and well fed," but does nothing about his physical needs, what good is it? In the same way, faith by itself, if it is not accompanied by action, is dead.

But someone will say, "You have faith; I have deeds."

Show me your faith without deeds, and I will show you my faith by what I do. You believe that there is one God. Good! Even the demons believe that - and shudder.

You foolish man, do you want evidence that faith without deeds is useless? Was not our ancestor Abraham considered righteous for what he did when he offered his son Isaac on the altar? You see that his faith and his actions were working together, and his faith was made complete by what he did. And the scripture was fulfilled that says, "Abraham believed God, and it was credited to him as righteousness," and he was called God's friend. You see that a person is justified by what he does and not by faith alone.

In the same way, was not even Rahab the prostitute considered righteous for what she did when she gave lodging to the spies and sent them off in a different direction? As the body without the spirit is dead, so faith without deeds is dead.

There are times when God uses specific circumstances and individuals to illustrate specific truths. In a very real way, the prophet Isaiah and his family became such symbols as we read in Isaiah 7-8. <u>First, we read Isaiah 7:3:</u>

Then the LORD said to Isaiah, "Go out, you and your son <u>Shear-Jashub</u>, to meet Ahaz at the end of the aqueduct of the Upper Pool, on the road to the Washerman's Field.

The name Shear-Jashub is Hebrew meaning "a remnant shall return" and this boy became the prophetic declaration found in Isaiah 10:21-23:

A remnant will return, a remnant of Jacob

will return to the Mighty God.

Though your people, O Israel, be like the sand by the sea, only a remnant will return.

Destruction has been decreed,

overwhelming and righteous.

The Lord, the LORD Almighty, will carry out

the destruction decreed upon the whole land.

<u>Second, we read Isaiah 8:1 -4:</u>

The LORD said to me, "Take a large scroll and write on it with an ordinary pen: Maher-Shalal-Hash-Baz. And I will call in Uriah the priest and Zechariah son of Jeberekiah as reliable witnesses for me."

Then I went to the prophetess, and she conceived and gave birth to a son. And the LORD said to me, "Name him Maher-Shalal-Hash-Baz. Before the boy knows how to say 'My father' or 'My mother,' the wealth of Damascus and the plunder of Samaria will be carried off by the king of Assyria."

This strange name means "quick to the plunder; swift to the spoil." The names of these children became the prophetic word of judgment and restoration. That is why Isaiah spoke the words written in Isaiah 8:18:

<u>Here am I, and the children the LORD has given me. We are signs and symbols in Israel from the LORD Almighty, who dwells on Mount Zion.</u>

In a similar way the personal life and marriage of the prophet Hosea became a visible symbol of the relationship between the Lord and his people. In the pain of Hosea, the pain of God became visibly displayed and in the unfaithfulness of his wife the unfaithfulness of Israel was shown. In a very real way Hosea learned the lesson about the incredible love of God for his people through his personal experience of his broken marriage.

Much of what I am trying to convey in this book was birthed during a time of what I can only describe as an incredibly difficult time in our lives and in the lives of a few individuals with whom we were privileged to walk on the journey of faith. Five years ago, in obedience to what the Lord had spoken to me, I walked out of the security of a regular and successful pastorate into a journey to live by faith. This has been an incredible journey and my wife and I have said many times that we would not have had it any other way. At the same time, we have walked through days when it seemed as if there was no light and no hope and all that kept us going was the deep conviction that we had heard from the Lord and he would never let us down.

This is not the place and time to relate details of the situation, but to focus on the key issue before us. As I reflected on the next leg of our journey of faith, I became aware of the fact that in a very real way our situation has become an illustration and a sign of this Kingdom reality, which I am trying to convey to you. Walking in obedience to what we heard from the Lord we found ourselves in a position of severe financial stress. In truth, it did not seem to make any sense to do what we were doing and like many we ourselves asked hard questions – yet all we heard from the Lord was to trust and continue to walk in faith.

However, we live in a society where believers can quote 2 Corinthians 5:7, "we live by faith, not by sight," but in truth most live by sight. In church we like to hear the stories of the heroes of faith like Abraham and how he continued to expect the birth of a son, even though Sarah had long passed the age to bear a child. It is great to preach a sermon on Abraham and to talk about a walk of faith in spite of the fact that everything in us says it makes no sense. It is easier to sit in judgment and to talk about the birthing of "Ishmaels" in ministry, than to walk the walk of faith. **As we walked this strange path in faith God told us very clearly that we are not to ask anyone (except one specific case) for financial help. We were simply to walk in faith. In time the need became very obvious and first of all to those who were the closest to us. As the need became known we saw and experienced the wide spectrum of responses to the need.**

First and foremost, there were those who were like the friends of Job. They came and sympathized for a little while and then shared their insights – from "possible secret and unconfessed sin" in our lives to "curses". The fact was that "everyone knows that if we are in the will of God we will prosper!" Thus, the conclusion of many was that we were either outside of the will of God or we have some unconfessed sin in our lives. Some shared what "God had told them about us" and in a polite way suggested that we could not have heard what we heard from the Lord. Having concluded that, all that remained was that we deal with the issues and we will be blessed. Thus, there was no need for these friends to respond further; for they had theologized and gave the logical answer that we obviously missed. At most we got a token response from a small minority of them. Life goes on and they had moved past us in a way that was not much different than the priest and the Levite in the parable. In time many simply ignored us, for it is easier to do that than to again be faced with the choice of a response or not.

On the other hand, there were those who did not have much – some in dire situations themselves, but they understood and gave what little they had. When our vehicle needed repairs that we could not afford, a couple simply brought their second vehicle over for as long as we would need it. They rejoiced as they responded and at other times they would just drop in with food, as did their neighbor. A very impoverished family gave a gift of cash from a blessing they had received. A widow and her daughter sent a gift, as did a single mom who for years has blessed us as personal intercessor. A friend dropped in one day to visit and picked up on the need, went home and with his wife paid an unpaid utility bill – with no questions asked. A small and financially strapped local church sent a liberal gift and the house churches went overboard in liberality as they responded to the need. A friend heard and was so troubled he could not sleep. He called me the next day and was in tears. Financially he was not in a position to help, but he felt the need and cried with me. Interestingly, he made the connection with the words quoted above from James 2:14-26 and said he felt convicted even though he was not able to respond. I was struck with his honesty and his agony and in the midst of our conversation God ministered to both of us. Even a man from another faith to whom we have witnessed reached out and shared how they respond to such needs in his faith community and it was as if he had read James 2.

Another friend came to our office one day. Some time back he was going through a very similar situation and even though he did all he could at the time, it was in vain. We had prayed and worked with him at the time and he did not forget. He came to pray a blessing upon us and to encourage us with his own story – how God literally stepped in the day he was to lose his house and provided in an unexpected way and how God continued to bless him so that in a short time his debts were paid. Having focused on paying his debts he had little to spare, but wanted to encourage us and pray with us. We joined hands with this carpenter and he prayed over us. It helped us so much and we thanked God for the visit.

The real fascinating part of the story involves another friend. Let us simply call him John. He is an affluent man and had been supporting us on an irregular basis through a number of years. As we entered into a very difficult time with growing need for financial support, we knew in the Spirit that John was to help us, but God told us very clearly that we were not to ask him. He dropped in from time to time and became well aware of the need, yet for some reason chose not to respond. Many months later God told me to visit him and talk to him about the matter, but only to clarify issues and not to ask for help. We talked very openly. John admitted that he knew he had to respond to the need, but because of misunderstanding and personal issues with another friend close to us he chose not to respond. These issues were clarified and the need was spelled out. It also became clear that we did have different views about support for Christian ministries. He felt I should pound the pavement, visit key business leaders, share the vision and ask for support – as other ministries did. I pointed out that much of that is very contrary to Scripture and also that I was explicitly told by the Lord not to do it. We read James 2:14- 26 together and talked at length about it, again very openly. I made it clear to him that God did not send me to him to ask for anything, simply to clarify the issues and to challenge him to look at his resources through Kingdom eyes and to especially pay attention to the passage in James 2.

After we had prayed together, I left. As I walked to the vehicle, he excitedly remembered a key businessman's name and suggested that I visit this man and ask for a donation. Laughingly I reminded John that I had just spent the better part of an hour sharing that God did not send me to find support in that way. Did he not hear me? He countered that he had just spent the same time suggesting to me what was in his opinion the better option and did I not listen? Looking him in the eye, I said: "I promise to pray about it and you do the same. If God tells me to visit this man and ask for support, I will do that.

However, if God tells you to go on my behalf, then you do it!" We had a good visit and shared openly, but John did not make any effort to respond to the need. I was puzzled, especially as he was the only one to whom God specifically sent me to talk about the issues.

A number of weeks later we faced a very specific need with a very definite deadline and no way to meet the need. Again, God was very clear in his direction to us that we were not to ask anyone, but simply to pray and seek him. We were led to ask a small number of people to pray specifically for the need with us. We were very careful to keep that only to those that God had revealed. They were people who were not able to personally meet the need, except to support us in prayer. As we continued to pray with no breakthrough even remotely in sight and an increasingly tight timeline, God told me to visit John again. This time I was to specifically ask him to meet the need. Having heard this, I went to see John and shared the need asking him to pray about it. He was very open as I spoke to him and as I told him that I was released to ask him. I also reminded him that that was precisely the way he suggested I should follow as general rule to get support for the ministry needs. With a very short timeline, I waited a number of days and then called to hear his answer. John said he had the funds, but still was not sure. I replied that I understood and when he knew the answer to contact me. The deadline came and went – God brought relief through others (a real miracle) and the need was met, but to this day John has not come back to me.

I was again puzzled as to why God had sent me to John in the first place. As I said, he was the only person God released me to visit, to challenge and finally to ask for the specific need. Yet through it all he did not respond. Then I heard the Lord say to me: "You did not miss it at all. First, for you it is to be a confirmation that you are right that the way most ministries raise support is not my way at all. You could have milked John for great donations and manipulated offerings in the way many do. But this is the confirmation to you that it is not to be done. However, for John it was a test. In fact, I spoke to him three times now about the need to support you. First, he ignored it, because he had misunderstandings and chose to give the funds to someone else and then excused himself that he had given. Then I sent you to clear up the misunderstandings and to make the need known. In the process he read the words in James 2 and it was evident what needed to be done. Again, he chose not to respond for he insisted that you follow his way and ask. Thus, I sent you again and this time he listened to the need and **according to his own rules he was asked** – and yet again he chose not to respond. Three times I spoke to him and three times he refused to listen!" **Let him who has ears listen to the Spirit!**

I know this is getting too close for many! However, this is the truth. The church in the Western world has lost sight of the fact that our faith does not need buildings and programs. **We are called to be people of The Way, compelled by the love of God in Christ.** It is interesting to read the story of those who were first known as people of The Way as described in the book of Acts. It is especially interesting when we remember that compared to us, they were for the most part not wealthy and they did not have the infra structure we seem to think is absolutely necessary for a church. They did not have buildings and programs. They did not have committees and benevolence funds handled by a few on behalf of the rest. Let us read Acts 2:42-47:

They devoted themselves to the apostles' teaching and to the fellowship, to the breaking of bread and to prayer. Everyone was filled with awe, and many wonders and miraculous signs were done by the apostles. <u>All the believers were together and had everything in common. Selling their possessions and goods, they gave to anyone as he had need.</u> Every day they continued to meet together in the temple courts. They broke bread in their homes and ate together with glad and sincere hearts, praising God and enjoying the favor of all the people. And the Lord added to their number daily those who were being saved.

No matter how we want to interpret these words, they cared for one another with a willingness to give to those in need, even if it cost them! A few chapters later we read Acts 4:32-37:

<u>All the believers were one in heart and mind. No one claimed that any of his possessions was his own, but they shared everything they had.</u> With great power the apostles continued to testify to the resurrection of the Lord Jesus, and much grace was upon them all. <u>There were no needy persons among them.</u> <u>For from time to time those who owned lands or houses sold</u>

them, brought the money from the sales and put it at the apostles' feet, and it was distributed to anyone as he had need.

Joseph, a Levite from Cyprus, whom the apostles called Barnabas (which means Son of Encouragement), sold a field he owned and brought the money and put it at the apostles' feet.

Let us take note of the way these early believers walked in The Way. They did not set up a benevolence fund with special offerings. They did not have a committee to discuss and "discreetly" handle matters like these. Benevolence was not just another program in the church, for they did not have programs! They did not have budgets and the vast majority of their funds were not spent in the building and upkeep of huge buildings called "churches" with programs directed by a special class called clergy. They walked in relationship and where there was a need they responded with generosity and joy. Homes were open for that was where they met for the most part and hospitality was part and parcel of The Way. They had no support from the government and no one needed the incentive of a tax receipt to make a donation. They walked in a freedom and generosity compelled by the love of God that they encountered in Christ and this love was manifested in his body known as the people of The Way.

E.g. Hebrews 13:1-3, 1 John 3:16-20 and 1 John 4:7-12:

Keep on loving each other as brothers. Do not forget to entertain strangers, for by so doing some people have entertained angels without knowing it. Remember those in prison as if you were their fellow prisoners, and those who are mistreated as if you yourselves were suffering.

<u>This is how we know what love is: Jesus Christ laid down his life for us. And we ought to lay down our lives for our brothers. If anyone has material possessions and sees his brother in need but has no pity on him, how can the love of God be in him? Dear children, let us not love with words or tongue but with actions and in truth.</u> This then is how we know that we belong to the truth, and how we set our hearts at rest in his presence whenever our hearts condemn us. For God is greater than our hearts, and he knows everything.

Dear friends, let us love one another, for love comes from God. Everyone who loves has been born of God and knows God. Whoever does not love does not know God, because God is love. This is how God showed his love among us: He sent his one and only Son into the world that we might live through him. This is love: not that we loved God, but that he loved us and sent his Son as an atoning sacrifice for our sins. <u>Dear friends, since God so loved us, we also ought to love one another. No one has ever seen God; but if we love one another, God lives in us and his love is made complete in us.</u>

As we close this chapter it is fitting to read a story of how the love of Christ compelled a woman into extravagant generosity. It is found in every one of the four gospels, each time with a special emphasis. Let us read Mark 14:3-9:

While he was in Bethany, reclining at the table in the home of a man known as Simon the leper, a woman came with an alabaster jar of very expensive perfume, made of pure nard. She broke the jar and poured the perfume on his head.

Some of those present were saying indignantly to one another, "Why this waste of perfume? It could have been sold for more than a year's wages and the money given to the poor." And they rebuked her harshly.

"Leave her alone," said Jesus. "Why are you bothering her? She has done a beautiful thing to me. The poor you will always have with you, and you can help them any time you want. But you will not always have me. She did what she could. She poured perfume on my body beforehand to prepare for my burial. I tell you the truth, wherever the gospel is preached throughout the world, what she has done will also be told, in memory of her."

In one moment, a year's wages were wasted in an act of extravagant love as the jar was broken and the contents poured out. With that act this former prostitute poured out her deepest love and appreciation for the gift of the Father in Christ and for the love she experienced as he healed her and set her free. Yes – logic and common sense said this gift could have been handled in a different way, but as Jesus said that day, nearly 2000 years later this story is still fresh and speaking to us in memory of her.

The poor are still here with us today, too! The needs are all around and this same Jesus is showing up in and through them as he said. He does this for he is currently interceding for us. That is why he came to the world and gave his life. Most believers know the wonderful prophetic words of Isaiah 53 where the suffering of Christ was predicted hundreds of years before the fullness of time. The end of this passage reads as follows, Isaiah 53:11-12:

After the suffering of his soul, he will see the light [of life] and be satisfied; by his knowledge my righteous servant will justify many, and he will bear their iniquities.

Therefore, I will give him a portion among the great, and he will divide the spoils with the strong, <u>because he poured out his life unto death, and was numbered with the transgressors.</u>

<u>*For he bore the sin of many, and made intercession for the transgressors.*</u>

Jesus Christ came to this world to become one of us. He was willing to be in the number with us and identify with us, even though he was the only one who did not sin. This is why he is able to make intercession for us as Isaiah prophesied. Hebrews 7:23-25:

Now there have been many of those priests, since death prevented them from continuing in office; but because Jesus lives forever, he has a permanent priesthood. Therefore, he is able to save completely those who come to God through him, because he always lives to intercede for them. (See also Romans 8:3).

The word "intercede" means to speak on behalf of someone, even to ask something for someone else. The picture is that Jesus, even though he had no sin, chose to be identified with us as sinners and with our needs. He is able to sympathize with us and lives to support us in our petitions to the Father. He pleads our case as our brother with the Father, or as Scripture says, "he lives to intercede for us." **In the very same way, he enters into our presence as intercessor at times on behalf of a brother or sister in need. That is the heart of the message he spoke in Matthew 25:31 - 6:1 that we quoted earlier.**

What if I cannot personally meet the need? In the center of his teaching on prayer recorded in Luke 11:1-13 Jesus illustrated this point with a simple story, Luke 11:5-10:

Then he said to them, "Suppose one of you has a friend, and he goes to him at midnight and says, 'Friend, lend me three loaves of bread, because a friend of mine on a journey has come to me, and I have nothing to set before him.'

"Then the one inside answers, 'Don't bother me. The door is already locked, and my children are with me in bed. I can't get up and give you anything.' I tell you, though he will not get up and give him the bread because he is his friend, yet because of the man's boldness he will get up and give him as much as he needs.

"So, I say to you: Ask and it will be given to you; seek and you will find; knock and the door will be opened to you. For everyone who asks receives; he who seeks finds; and to him who knocks, the door will be opened."

The friend is the intercessor. He finds himself in a position where he sees a need and is unable to personally meet the need. However, he sets out even at an inopportune time and knocks on the door of a neighbor to get the need met for the person in need. This is what the Kingdom is all about! It is about being compelled by the love of Christ to meet the needs of people or going the extra mile to make sure the needs are being met. It is about recognizing Jesus when he steps into our lives in the person whose need is revealed and responding by reaching out with spontaneous extravagance – with a reckless freedom to break through the bottle neck of fear of lack by grasping the principles of being a steward of Kingdom resources. It is time to take a closer look at the stewardship in the Kingdom.

THE KING'S RESOURCES

One of the main issues to settle in our minds and in our hearts, centers on our claims to ownership of resources. In this we are no different than the people of Israel were. This was the context of the well-known parable of the talents recorded in Matthew 25:14-30:

"Again, it will be like a man going on a journey, who called his servants and entrusted his property to them. To one he gave five talents of money, to another two talents, and to another one talent, each according to his ability. Then he went on his journey. The man who had received the five talents went at once and put his money to work and gained five more. So also, the one with the two talents gained two more. But the man who had received the one talent went off, dug a hole in the ground and hid his master's money.

After a long time, the master of those servants returned and settled accounts with them. The man who had received the five talents brought the other five. 'Master,' he said, 'you entrusted me with five talents. See, I have gained five more.'

His master replied, 'Well done, good and faithful servant! You have been faithful with a few things; I will put you in charge of many things. Come and share your master's happiness!'

The man with the two talents also came. 'Master,' he said, 'you entrusted me with two talents; see, I have gained two more.'

His master replied, 'Well done, good and faithful servant! You have been faithful with a few things; I will put you in charge of many things. Come and share your master's happiness!'

Then the man who had received the one talent came. 'Master,' he said, 'I knew that you are a hard man, harvesting where you have not sown and gathering where you have not scattered seed. So, I was afraid and went out and hid your talent in the ground. See, here is what belongs to you.'

His master replied, 'You wicked, lazy servant! So, you knew that I harvest where I have not sown and gather where I have not scattered seed? Well then, you should have put my money on deposit with the bankers, so that when I returned, I would have received it back with interest.

'Take the talent from him and give it to the one who has the ten talents. For everyone who has will be given more, and he will have an abundance. Whoever does not have, even what he has will be taken from him. And throw that worthless servant outside, into the darkness, where there will be weeping and gnashing of teeth.'"

Without discussing this in detail, let us note the obvious points. This parable deals with the issue of stewardship in the Kingdom. **The resources belong to the King. These are entrusted to us according to our abilities and we are accountable to the King for the way in which we handle these resources. It is very important to read the sobering words of the apostle Paul to Timothy in 1 Timothy 6:7:**

For we brought nothing into the world, and we can take nothing out of it.

In the Kingdom of God all the resources belong to God. You and I are simply stewards entrusted with the care of the resources. However, as we enter the Kingdom through faith in Jesus, we find that the King is also our Father! We do not simply become stewards of the royal resources, but we have become children of the King and as children we have full access to the resources. Thus, we can walk in The Way as outlined by Jesus in Matthew 6:19-34:

Do not store up for yourselves treasures on earth, where moth and rust destroy, and where thieves break in and steal. But store up for yourselves treasures in heaven, where moth and rust do not destroy, and where thieves do not break in and steal. For where your treasure is, there your heart will be also.

The eye is the lamp of the body. If your eyes are good, your whole body will be full of light. But if your eyes are bad, your whole body will be full of darkness. If then the light within you is darkness, how great is that darkness!

No one can serve two masters. Either he will hate the one and love the other, or he will be devoted to the one and despise the other. You cannot serve both God and Money.

Therefore. I tell you, do not worry about your life, what you will eat or drink; or about your body, what you will wear. Is not life more important than food, and the body more important than clothes? Look at the birds of the air; they do not sow or reap or store away in barns, and yet your heavenly Father feeds them. Are you not much more valuable than they? Who of you by worrying can add a single hour to his life?

And why do you worry about clothes? See how the lilies of the field grow. They do not labor or spin. Yet I tell you that not even Solomon in all his splendor was dressed like one of these. If that is how God clothes the grass of the field, which is here today and tomorrow is thrown into the fire, will he not much more clothe you, O you of little faith? So do not worry, saying, 'What shall we eat?' or 'What shall we drink?' or 'What shall we wear?' For the pagans run after all these things, and your heavenly Father knows that you need them. But seek first his kingdom and his righteousness, and all these things will be given to you as well. Therefore, do not worry about tomorrow, for tomorrow will worry about itself. Each day has enough trouble of its own.

There is a tremendous freedom that comes through knowing that in Christ we have received full access to the Father and we can trust him to care for us. It is the key that opens the door for us to walk in The Way. It allows us to see the world through Kingdom focused eyes and to seek first the Kingdom and his righteousness – without worrying about financial issues. **However, do not miss the key point here: you cannot serve God and money. There can only be one master and the King will not share his throne with any other god, particularly with money!**

This brings us to the story of the man we call "the rich young ruler." The story is found in Luke 18:18-30:

A certain ruler asked him, "Good teacher, what must I do to inherit eternal life?"

"Why do you call me good?" Jesus answered. "No one is good-except God alone. You know the commandments: 'Do not commit adultery, do not murder, do not steal, do not give false testimony, honor your father and mother.'"

"All these I have kept since I was a boy," he said.

When Jesus heard this, he said to him, "You still lack one thing. Sell everything you have and give to the poor, and you will have treasure in heaven. Then come, follow me." When he heard this, he became very sad, because he was a man of great wealth. Jesus looked at him and said, "How hard it is for the rich to enter the kingdom of God! Indeed, it is easier for a camel to go through the eye of a needle than for a rich man to enter the kingdom of God."

Those who heard this asked, "Who then can be saved?"

<u>Jesus replied, "What is impossible with men is possible with God."</u>

Peter said to him, "We have left all we had to follow you!"

"I tell you the truth," Jesus said to them, "no one who has left home or wife or brothers or parents or children for the sake of the kingdom of God will fail to receive many times as much in this age and, in the age to come, eternal life."

Normally we explain the meaning of the passage in such a way that it really does not apply to any of us. We try to take the radical challenge away. **However, this is the measure of the Kingdom of God and a key to walking in the Way!** The Old Covenant taught the principle of tithing. "The New Covenant says we do not give God a measly 10% of what we get, we give it all to him." (Michael Wood from Australia said this to me as we talked a while back.) **Listen: You will never live the Kingdom lifestyle without dealing with this issue in a radical way. You will never understand the freedom offered in Christ fully if you do not face the issue of materialism in your life. This story was not recorded to challenge a few whom we consider to be rich. It is the very heart of our faith.**

When Jesus called his twelve disciples, they left everything to follow him. This is why Peter spoke as he did when the rich young ruler walked away. During their walk with him as they learned The Way, e.g. when Jesus sent them out to do the work of the Kingdom and gave them specific commands as we read in Matthew 10:5-16:

These twelve Jesus sent out with the following instructions: "Do not go among the Gentiles or enter any town of the

Samaritans. Go rather to the lost sheep of Israel. <u>As you go, preach this message: 'The kingdom of heaven is near.' Heal the sick, raise the dead, cleanse those who have leprosy, drive out demons. Freely you have received, freely give. Do not take along any gold or silver or copper in your belts; take no bag for the journey, or extra tunic, or sandals or a staff; for the worker is worth his keep.</u>

Whatever town or village you enter, search for some worthy person there and stay at his house until you leave. As you enter the home, give it your greeting. If the home is deserving, let your peace rest on it; if it is not, let your peace return to you. If anyone will not welcome you or listen to your words, shake the dust off your feet when you leave that home or town. I tell you the truth; it will be more bearable for Sodom and Gomorrah on the day of judgment than for that town. I am sending you out like sheep among wolves. Therefore, be as shrewd as snakes and as innocent as doves.

Did you note that the workers were not to take anything? However, they were to expect that their needs would be met. **To walk in The Way, one needs to have a simple faith that the Father will meet our daily needs. The disciples were to give freely in ministry for they had received freely. These words are a key to the Kingdom Way of life. Those to whom the messengers came were given an opportunity to receive them and to respond to their needs with hospitality and support. Failing to do that brought judgment upon them.**

Just prior to his ascension Jesus spoke to them again and gave them what we term "the great commission," Matthew 28:18-20:

"All authority in heaven and on earth has been given to me. Therefore, go and make disciples of all nations, baptizing them in the name of the Father and of the Son and of the Holy Spirit, and teaching them to obey everything I have commanded you. And surely, I am with you always, to the very end of the age."

Included in the words "to obey everything he had commanded them", is the teaching that to walk in The Way one has to let go of everything. Once you understand the Kingdom vision nothing else is worth hanging on to. Jesus explained this to his disciples through two short parables recorded in Matthew 13:44-46:

The kingdom of heaven is like treasure hidden in a field. When a man found it, he hid it again, and then in his joy went and sold all he had and bought that field.

Again, the kingdom of heaven is like a merchant looking for fine pearls. When he found one of great value, he went away and sold everything he had and bought it.

This principle was illustrated in and through Jesus himself. He is our example and his life revealed the Way of the Kingdom. In the words of Philippians 2:5-8:

Your attitude should be the kind that was shown us by Jesus Christ, who, though he was God, did not demand and cling to his rights as God, but laid aside his mighty power and glory, taking the disguise of a slave and becoming like men.

And he humbled himself even further, going so far as actually to die a criminal's death on a cross. TLB

In order to reveal the Kingdom of God to us, Jesus chose to let go of all that he had and gave it up willingly for us. Once human he continued to walk in The Way even giving up his life for us on a cross. In the words of 2 Corinthians 8:8-9:

For you know the grace of our Lord Jesus Christ, that though he was rich, yet for your sakes he became poor, so that you through his poverty might become rich.

This is the essential message of the Good News of the Kingdom. The God of this universe was willing to give everything he had so that we might be restored into fellowship with him and enjoy his presence and care. The first believers understood this very well. Peter and the other disciples gave everything up to follow him. When they began preaching the message of the Kingdom, we read how those who came to faith walked in The Way and when it came to possessions, we read Acts 4:32:

All the believers were one in heart and mind. No one claimed that any of his possessions was his own, but they shared everything they had.

They were able to share with others and meet the needs of those less fortunate. Walking in The Way meant meeting needs and caring. This was nowhere better illustrated than when there was a specific need in Judea and special relief funds were gathered from the churches and sent to help in the need. In this regard Paul wrote to the Corinthians and mentioned the fact that there was an amazing generosity shown by the poorer churches in Macedonia, 2 Corinthians 8:1-15:

And now, brothers, we want you to know about the grace that God has given the Macedonian churches. Out of the most severe trial, their overflowing joy and their extreme poverty welled up in rich generosity. For I testify that they gave as much as they were able, and even beyond their ability. Entirely on their own, they urgently pleaded with us for the privilege of sharing in this service to the saints. And they did not do as we expected, but they gave themselves first to the Lord and then to us in keeping with God's will. So, we urged Titus, since he had earlier made a beginning, to bring also to completion this act of grace on your part. But just as you excel in everything - in faith, in speech, in knowledge, in complete earnestness and in your love for us - see that you also excel in this grace of giving.

I am not commanding you, but I want to test the sincerity of your love by comparing it with the earnestness of others. For you know the grace of our Lord Jesus Christ, that though he was rich, yet for your sakes he became poor, so that you through his poverty might become rich.

And here is my advice about what is best for you in this matter: Last year you were the first not only to give but also to have the desire to do so. Now finish the work, so that your eager willingness to do it may be matched by your completion of it, according to your means. For if the willingness is there, the gift is acceptable according to what one has, not according to what he does not have.

Our desire is not that others might be relieved while you are hard pressed, but that there might be equality. <u>At the present time your plenty will supply what they need, so that in turn their plenty will supply what you need.</u> Then there will be equality, as it is written: "He who gathered much did not have too much, and he who gathered little did not have too little."

Note the key to the generosity of the poor believers in Macedonia: They gave themselves first to the Lord. Their generosity flowed out of their love for the Lord. They were no different than the lady who broke her vase to pour the expensive oil on Jesus as a spontaneous act of extravagant love. Let us return to that story for a moment and read some of the detail as recorded in Luke 7:39-47:

When the Pharisee who had invited him saw this, he said to himself, "If this man were a prophet, he would know who is touching him and what kind of woman she is - that she is a sinner."

Jesus answered him, "Simon, I have something to tell you."

"Tell me, teacher," he said.

"Two men owed money to a certain moneylender. One owed him five hundred denarii, and the other fifty. Neither of

them had the money to pay him back, so he canceled the debts of both. Now which of them will love him more?"

Simon replied, "I suppose the one who had the bigger debt canceled."

"You have judged correctly," Jesus said.

Then he turned toward the woman and said to Simon, "Do you see this woman? I came into your house. You did not give me any water for my feet, but she wet my feet with her tears and wiped them with her hair. You did not give me a kiss, but this woman, from the time I entered, has not stopped kissing my feet. You did not put oil on my head, but she has poured perfume on my feet. Therefore, I tell you, her many sins have been forgiven - for she loved much. But he who has been forgiven little loves little."

Earlier I shared how we were put in a position where we had never been and how God not only used us as a prophetic example to many who know us, but taught us about these matters in very real ways. As we walked this strange path, we noticed two kinds of givers in the body of Christ – apart from the majority who never learned to give! There are two kinds of givers: First those who give from the overflow. They are true givers. They care and they give, but it comes from the overflow. They first take care of themselves and their perceived needs (often not real needs). When they are blessed, they will share with others and often liberally, but it does not cost them much if any. They are like the businessmen who have a set formula – and if the amount in the budget for "charity" is spent, then further requests have to wait till the next year's budget. **The second kind of giver is rare, for in our society true Kingdom vision is very limited.** This kind of giver is the one who will spontaneously break the vase and go overboard – even if it costs everything. The first are the "tithers" and the second the Kingdom givers. The first are satisfied and feel good if they give a tithe to the local church and an occasional offering above and beyond the tithe. The second are the ones who will go the extra mile and who know the joy of giving till it hurts, for they understand the Way of the Cross. The first are the ones who are serious about their faith, but the second are the ones who are willing to be radical and who will take the radical challenge of Jesus seriously.

It is time to connect a few dots and get the picture. In the Western world and particularly here in North America we have cut the heart out of the radical message of the Kingdom. We have made it into a structure that is very different from The Way. In truth, our churches operate like the temple in the days of Jesus. The Jewish religious leaders made the temple user friendly by making it easy for the people to fulfill the requirements of the sacrificial laws. They had the approved sacrifices available on the premises for a fee and it also served to increase the revenue at the temple. It was much easier to travel with money to the temple and buy the approved animal there than bringing an animal over a long distance and run the risk of finding that it did not pass the test. Our churches are also very user friendly and set up to accommodate our giving. We print envelopes (even have ATMs and electronic debit and credit machines) and have the added incentive of tax receipts – so all we need is to pass the offering plate or basket. Once in a while we take a special offering for benevolence or for mission or the local food bank – thus relieving the members of the church from any sense of listening to the Spirit about the need of a brother or sister. We do not expect to have Jesus come to us as he had said in Matthew 25 – for he should know better and approach the benevolence committee. After all, that is their job and we elected or appointed them to look after these kinds of things. **The problem is that the church's response to real need flow from structure and not from true compassion!** Moreover, the needs at our modern temples are great for we have to spend large sums of money to get the property and facilities that will attract the right people to our church. Then we need the right pastoral staff to do the ministry and run the programs that will keep them coming and that costs money, brother! We do care for the lost; that is why we are seeker sensitive in our approach and programs. **We cannot afford to be radical and if those with major resources simply begin to listen to the Spirit and give where they see need, it will constitute a similar threat to the church that Jesus did when he turned the tables upside down and took the whip to the merchants in the temple. Jesus would never do that to our church, or would he?**

Let me challenge you to read the New Testament again. It is a radical message of Good News of the Kingdom. It is the message about the extravagant love of God for the world. This love was radically displayed in the life and death and resurrection of the man called Jesus of Nazareth. The New Testament is the message of people who responded to this love by walking in this radical way with an authenticity that we rarely see in our society. They were known as the people of The Way, because they had a radical lifestyle that set them apart from all others in society. They were like the merchant who found the pearl of great price and sold all to get that one pearl. They dealt with the issue of possessions and settled it, for they heard the voice of Jesus and knew he spoke the truth when he said that you couldn't serve God and money. They knew it was true that where their treasure is there their heart will be, so they chose to seek first his Kingdom and its righteousness. They heard him speak about money and possessions more than almost any other subject for the simple reason that the way they handled these things would have a major impact on their faith.

In the introduction I said that as we move into the dawn of this Third Day our Lord Jesus is getting ready to perfect his body, the Church. We are entering into a time when we will witness the greatest Reformation the church has ever seen. This new Reformation will come about, as the truth of the priesthood of the believer will be restored as it was in the early years of the church. One of the first signs of this reformation will be the breaking of the control over the Kingdom resources by the established church and its hierarchy. Currently the vast majority of the Kingdom resources are wasted in ineffective programs, in the erection and upkeep of buildings and in the salaries of the staff that fail to release the believers into their ministry because of their insecurity and to keep their jobs. **As the truth of the priesthood of the believer begins to be heard and received the landscape of the church will be radically changed. As believers begin to walk in The Way they will use their gifts and resources in productive ways and invest in ordinary people with a true Kingdom mindset instead of in churches and programs focused on maintaining ineffective and self-serving purposes. They will begin to see the Lord as he comes in the needs of people and respond with a generosity and extravagance that will astound the world as it did in the early years of the church. Being the church ordinary people will walk in an anointing that will manifest in miracles, healing and deliverance – and it will happen without a superstar traveling in a jet with a large entourage to handle the logistics of the crowds.**

It is time to connect some more dots and see the picture in sharper detail. In the previous chapter I shared the story of my friend John and his struggle to respond to the challenge of our personal needs. Three times he was confronted and three times he found a reason to ignore the need. He has been a giver and generous with the overflow. He is standing at the edge of becoming a Kingdom giver and in time will move there. However, for now he has not been able to move to the point of extravagant love and releasing his resources for the sake of the Kingdom. Three times the risen Lord came to him and he failed to respond and acknowledge him – not unlike Peter in the gospel story. In my heart I know there is a day coming when my friend John will again meet the risen Lord and like Peter in John 21, he will be challenged (even three times if necessary) and he will become what God called him to be – a shepherd caring for the sheep.

It is all about the Kingdom and recognizing that everything belongs to the King. We are only stewards and when he calls on us to release his resources in our care to meet a need, we can do that with joy. The people of The Way had no problem to do this as we read in the Book of Acts for *"all the believers were one in heart and mind. No one claimed that any of his possessions was his own, but they shared everything they had."* They had settled the issue of possessions and had a freedom to meet the needs of others. There is also the wonderful freedom to rejoice with others that are being blessed instead of being jealous, for our King is generous and often blesses people in ways that does not make logical sense – e.g. Matthew 20:1-16:

For the kingdom of heaven is like a landowner who went out early in the morning to hire men to work in his vineyard. He agreed to pay them a denarius for the day and sent them into his vineyard.

About the third hour he went out and saw others standing in the marketplace doing nothing. He told them, 'You also go and work in my vineyard, and I will pay you whatever is right.' So, they went.

He went out again about the sixth hour and the ninth hour and did the same thing. About the eleventh hour he went out and found still others standing around. He asked them, 'Why have you been standing here all day long doing nothing?'

'Because no one has hired us,' they answered.

He said to them, 'You also go and work in my vineyard.'

When evening came, the owner of the vineyard said to his foreman, 'Call the workers and pay them their wages, beginning with the last ones hired and going on to the first.'

The workers who were hired about the eleventh hour came and each received a denarius. So, when those came who were hired first, they expected to receive more. But each one of them also received a denarius. When they received it, they began to grumble against the landowner. 'These men who were hired last worked only one hour,' they said, 'and you have made them equal to us who have borne the burden of the work and the heat of the day.' But he answered one of them, 'Friend, I am not being unfair to you. Didn't you agree to work for a denarius? Take your pay and go. I want to give the man who was hired last the same as I gave you. <u>Don't I have the right to do what I want with my own money? Or are you envious because I am generous?'</u>

So, the last will be first, and the first will be last.

Many years ago, the man called Jesus spoke about the Kingdom of God and illustrated The Way as he walked with a freedom like no one else. He did not merely come to speak about the Kingdom, but in a very real way he came to find the fruit from the King's vineyard as he said in Matthew 21:33-46:

"Listen to another parable: There was a landowner who planted a vineyard. He put a wall around it, dug a winepress in it and built a watchtower. Then he rented the vineyard to some farmers and went away on a journey. When the harvest time approached, he sent his servants to the tenants to collect his fruit.

The tenants seized his servants; they beat one, killed another, and stoned a third. Then he sent other servants to them, more than the first time, and the tenants treated them the same way. Last of all, he sent his son to them. 'They will respect my son,' he said.

But when the tenants saw the son, they said to each other, 'This is the heir. Come, let's kill him and take his inheritance.' So, they took him and threw him out of the vineyard and killed him.

Therefore, when the owner of the vineyard comes, what will he do to those tenants?"

"He will bring those wretches to a wretched end," they replied, "and he will rent the vineyard to other tenants, who will give him his share of the crop at harvest time."

Jesus said to them, "Have you never read in the Scriptures:

> *'The stone the builders rejected*
>
> *has become the capstone;*
>
> *the Lord has done this,*
>
> *and it is marvelous in our eyes'?*

Therefore' I tell you that the kingdom of God will be taken away from you and given to a people who will produce its fruit. He who falls on this stone will be broken to pieces, but he on whom it falls will be crushed."

When the chief priests and the Pharisees heard Jesus' parables, they knew he was talking about them. They looked for a way to arrest him, but they were afraid of the crowd because the people held that he was a prophet.

In Jesus the Father sent his son to collect the fruit from the vineyard. He came to the people to whom he entrusted the Kingdom, but they had assumed ownership over what was entrusted to them. He challenged them, particularly the leadership, about these matters and how they had rejected the words spoken by the prophets. Jesus then prophesied that he as the son would likewise be rejected and put to death. In a very real way, the Kingdom was taken from the people of Israel and given to the Gentiles according to the word of Jesus. In this process we as Gentiles have become the new tenants and we are to bring forth the fruit of the Kingdom for the King. In North America in particular there has been little fruit from the vineyard for the owner and when his son shows up to knock on the door for bread to feed a hungry brother or sister, he is sent away empty handed in most cases. The new tenants have again taken possession of the vineyard just like the leaders of Israel did in Jesus' days. The talents given to the many are used for personal gain to build local kingdoms that are conveniently called "churches" or "ministries", but instead of the Kingdom focus these are driven with a possessive vision not unlike that of the Pharisees and Sadducees of old. As I wrote in "Restoring the broken foundations," insecure leaders unwilling to release the members into ministry currently bury most of the talents of God's people in the pews. Most of the resources entrusted for Kingdom purposes are squandered to build and to maintain inefficient and underused buildings where the people of God are reduced to the status of spectators. These spectators are important as contributors through tithes and offerings to support the local kingdom and pay the salaries of the leaders who function in positions not sanctioned by Scripture. Those whose gifts "are being released" are for the most part used to fill slots in the program to maintain the status quo. They run the inefficient programs to keep the religious system running. This is vastly different than the picture presented in the New Testament where leadership and ministry touched and transformed the local society as they walked in The Way. It is time to connect a few more dots and see the picture of leadership walking in The Way.

SERVANT LEADERS

The new reformation will radically change the way leadership functions in the body of Christ. These issues are discussed in more detail in the book "Restoring the Broken Foundations", but it is important to get the main points in order to connect the dots. The Kingdom model that Jesus set in place was the model of servant leadership. One of his greatest struggles was to get the message of servant leadership through to his disciples. This is very clear as we read Matthew 20:20-28:

Then the mother of Zebedee's sons came to Jesus with her sons and, kneeling down, asked a favor of him.

"What is it you want?" he asked.

She said, "Grant that one of these two sons of mine may sit at your right and the other at your left in your kingdom."

"You don't know what you are asking," Jesus said to them. "Can you drink the cup I am going to drink?"

"We can," they answered.

Jesus said to them, "You will indeed drink from my cup, but to sit at my right or left is not for me to grant. These places belong to those for whom they have been prepared by my Father."

When the ten heard about this, they were indignant with the two brothers. Jesus called them together and said, "You know that the rulers of the Gentiles lord it over them, and their high officials exercise authority over them. Not so with you. <u>Instead, whoever wants to become great among you must be your servant, and whoever wants to be first must be your slave - just as the Son of Man did not come to be served, but to serve, and to give his life as a ransom for many."</u>

As the church is restored and foundations re-laid, the concept of servant leaders will be part and parcel of The Way. Leadership in the church is not a matter of titles and positions, but of service manifesting in fruit. But what is the fruit that comes from authentic Kingdom leadership? The answer is found in Ephesians 4:7-16:

But to each one of us grace has been given as Christ apportioned it. This is why it says:

> *"When he ascended on high,*
>
> *he led captives in his train*
>
> *and gave gifts to men."*

(What does "he ascended" mean except that he also descended to the lower, earthly regions? He who descended is the very one who ascended higher than all the heavens, in order to fill

the whole universe.) <u>It was he who gave some to be apostles, some to be prophets, some to be evangelists, and some to be pastors and teachers, to prepare God's people for works of service, so that the body of Christ may be built up until we all reach unity in the faith and in the knowledge of the Son of God and become mature, attaining to the whole measure of the fullness of Christ.</u>

Then we will no longer be infants, tossed back and forth by the waves, and blown here and there by every wind of teaching and by the cunning and craftiness of men in their deceitful scheming. Instead, speaking the truth in love, we will in all things grow up into him who is the Head, that is, Christ. From him the whole body, joined and held together by every supporting ligament, grows and builds itself up in love, as each part does its work.

The proof of Kingdom leadership is seen in the equipping of the saints for the work of ministry. True Kingdom leaders equip others and release them into ministry according to their gifts. The measure of the leadership is not measured by the size of the building or of the membership or budget, or by the programs that are being run. The measure of leadership is whether or not ordinary people are equipped and released to do the work of the ministry.

This brings us to the very interesting truth that needs to be pointed out: **The generally accepted role of "pastor" or "minister" as practiced in our churches has no foundation in Scripture**. In fact, the word only appears in this one reference in the New Testament (Ephesians

4:11). The Greek word is found in a number of passages in the rest of the New Testament, but mostly in reference to Jesus as "the shepherd." There are only two other references that can be quoted. The first is found in Acts 20 where it refers to the elders of the Church in Ephesus and Paul said to them in Acts 20:28:

Keep watch over yourselves and all the flock of which the Holy Spirit has made you overseers. <u>Be shepherds</u> of the church of God, which he bought with his own blood.

Keep watch over yourselves and all the flock of which the Holy Spirit has made you overseers. <u>Be shepherds</u> of the church of God, which he bought with his own blood.

In a similar sense Peter wrote 1 Peter 5:1-4:

To the elders among you, I appeal as a fellow elder, a witness of Christ's sufferings and one who also will share in the glory to be revealed: <u>Be shepherds</u> of God's flock that is under your care, serving as overseers - not because you must, but because you are willing, as God wants you to be; not greedy for money, but eager to serve; not lording it over those entrusted to you, but being examples to the flock. And when the Chief Shepherd appears, you will receive the crown of glory that will never fade away.

However, the references here are to a plurality of leaders who are the mature saints recognized by the church as leaders. **The current practice of "The Pastor" or "The Minister" as the spiritual leader of a local church has little or no foundation in Scripture.** The titles "Pastor,

Reverend and Minister" cannot be found in the New Testament and neither can the position represented by these titles be found in the New Testament. It is no wonder that the fruit of Kingdom leadership is lacking in our churches, for they represent a model of leadership that is contrary to what Jesus set in place for the church.

With that said, it is important to look at the leadership structure as set forth in Ephesians 4:7-16 quoted earlier. The risen Lord gave five leadership gifts to his body: Apostles, Prophets, Evangelists, Pastors and Teachers. As is clearly stated in this passage, the task of those called and anointed to function in these offices is to equip the members of the body for their work of ministry – period! The work of ministry is for every single member, for we are in the order of Melchizedek (described in the book "Ordinary People Extraordinary Royal Priests). This is the message of the Kingdom and clearly set forth in 1 Peter 2:4-10:

As you come to him, the living Stone - rejected by men but chosen by God and precious to him - you also, like living stones, are being built into a spiritual house to be a holy priesthood, offering spiritual sacrifices acceptable to God through Jesus Christ. For in Scripture it says:

> *"See, I lay a stone in Zion,*
>
> *a chosen and precious cornerstone,*
>
> *and the one who trusts in him will never be put to shame."*

Now to you who believe, this stone is precious. But to those who do not believe,

> *"The stone the builders rejected has become the capstone,"*

and,

> *"A stone that causes men to stumble and a rock that makes them fall."*

They stumble because they disobey the message - which is also what they were destined for.

<u>But you are a chosen people, a royal priesthood, a holy nation, a people belonging to God, that you may declare the praises of him who called you out of darkness into his wonderful light.</u> Once you were not a people, but now you are the people of God; once you had not received mercy, but now you have received mercy.

This is what the Third Day Church is all about. It is the people of God taking their place and doing the work of ministry. It is about God's people being released to walk in Kingdom authority and being the body of Jesus in the world. It is about God's people recognizing that they do not need to sit in pews and chairs and watch "the pastor" and "the leaders" doing the work of ministry while they "support" the ministry through tithes, offerings and helping to run the ineffective programs year in and year out. It is about God's people realizing that they do not need to have a special building for these programs to be part of the church, but that they are the church and called to ministry. It is about God's people recovering their roots in Christ and walking in The Way wherever they find themselves.

If we read the Bible and connect the dots, we will not find churches and steeples or pastors and programs. We will find ordinary people equipped by servant leaders and released into ministry <u>in the world.</u> We will find leaders who do not have titles, but who walk in authority that comes through relationship established in servant hood. They will know their call and anointing and those who have spiritual discernment will recognize them for who they are as gifts from Christ to his church.

Let us pinpoint a few more dots to connect about church leadership. According to Ephesians 4:12 there are five leadership gifts given by the risen Lord to his body, the church. In the last decades in particular this truth has been revealed anew to the church. Many talk about five-fold ministry. The truth that not only prophets, but also apostles, are gifts that did not disappear after the first century, is becoming accepted in more and more church circles. In the process we do face a major problem related to the fact that most try to fit this truth into the wrong model of what the church is! **Thus, apostles are mostly seen as those who plant churches according to the North American Levitical model. If this model were to be applied to the New Testament, we would conclude that no churches were planted at that time!**

This may sound strange to many and we need to look at it in more depth. On a personal level I have been involved in pastoring traditional churches for many years. I also helped to re-lay foundations in a traditional church that had gone through major power struggles. Then we moved into the world of independent charismatic churches and worked in church planting as part of a team (one without success and the other very successful). We learned the ropes from one of the most effective and qualified church planters of North American model churches in Canada. Following that God allowed us to be part of two independent charismatic churches, both functioning well according to North American standards and we experienced the view of the church from the position of "the laity". **In a word: We have been there and bought the T-shirts. In fact, if we take the T-shirts off, we have the scars to prove that we paid the price for every one of them!**

When God moved us out of the traditional church structure into the wonderful world of independent charismatic churches, we were excited to discover many truths that were new to us. We thank God for these things and for the privilege to move in the Spirit and for the gifts of the Spirit. We thank God for revealing the truth of the five-fold ministry gifts to us. When we began to work in the area of church planting, we recognized the need for apostles and prophets to lay the foundations, as is clear from 1 Corinthians 3:10- 11:

By the grace God has given me, <u>I laid a foundation as an expert builder</u>, and someone else is building on it. But each *one should be careful how he builds. For no one can lay any foundation other than the one already laid, which is Jesus Christ.*

Also, Ephesians 2:19-22:

Consequently, you are no longer foreigners and aliens, but fellow citizens with God's people and members of God's household, <u>built on the foundation of the apostles and prophets, with Christ Jesus himself as the chief cornerstone.</u> In him the whole building is joined together and rises to become a holy temple in the Lord. And in him you too are being built together to become a dwelling in which God lives by his Spirit.

The problem we discovered much later was that we had applied this truth to a model that is not found in Scripture, as the following will illustrate. The apostle (with or without a prophet!) would lay the foundation of the church as understood in the North American culture. So, we needed a church planting team and to launch the new church with success we also needed equipment. It is absolutely a must to have a worship leader and team with a sound system and equipment. The building is very important. It needs to be located in the right place and with the launching of the church proper advertising is vital. In addition to these the team must include leaders for the children's ministry and for youth. Without the latter there can be no church, for people who are used to church expect that. We also learned that there would be opposition – primarily from other established churches! After all, everyone has a staked claim to the territory and few understand that "we are not interested in stealing their members, but only in reaching the unchurched".

Let us stop here for a moment and seek the dots for this North American accepted picture in Scripture. As we read through the Book of Acts it is hard, no it is impossible, to find any mention of the need for a strategically located building with access to parking and for the necessary sound equipment. Paul seemed to have missed these classes on church planting and his teacher, Gamaliel, as well as the other apostles certainly did not understand the need for a worship leader and team and how vital a structured children's ministry is when you plant a church. Paul actually even ignored getting a qualified youth leader! The worst, however, is that he left the churches that he planted without appointing a pastor to do the work of ministry! Paul really seemed to believe that the local believers could do the ministry and be the church all on their own, for when he wrote the letters, he addressed these to the believers! Where there were issues to be sorted out or problems, he trusted that they could handle those without needing a pastor to make the decisions. There are no dots in Scripture to give us the picture of the "successful church planting methods" that we teach in North America! This would suggest that much of the North American teaching about apostles has to be reviewed in the light of Scripture.

So how did Paul plant churches? It would seem that wherever possible he started his mission in the local synagogues. He was a Jew and began with those who were close to his culture and who knew the Scripture of the Old Testament.

Using that he would reason with them while sharing the message of the Kingdom revealed in the Messiah, Jesus of Nazareth. Within the synagogue there were often Gentiles who were in process of converting to Judaism, called "God fearing men and women". Most of the time Paul's message would bring division, as some would accept it and others oppose it. Time and again he would be forced out of the synagogue, often persecuted and even forced out of town. On other occasions he would preach the gospel wherever he had opportunity – most of this in the street or marketplace. The preaching was not only in word, but also in deed, as sick were healed and demonic spirits cast out. Depending on the situation and time, Paul would stay from a short time to a year or more to establish the church. When he was able, he would return for a brief visit to review the progress and at times to appoint elders who were simply mature local leaders appointed to oversee the church. He also wrote letters to give advice, deal with problems and share news and information.

Paul never needed surveys and studies to determine the feasibility of a church plant in a town or region. He was first sent with the blessing of the Church in Antioch as we read in Acts 13:1-4:

In the church at Antioch there were prophets and teachers: Barnabas, Simeon called Niger, Lucius of Cyrene, Manaen (who had been brought up with Herod the tetrarch) and Saul. While they were worshiping the Lord and fasting, the Holy Spirit said, "Set apart for me Barnabas and Saul for the work to which I have called them." So, after they had fasted and prayed, they placed their hands on them and sent them off.

The two of them, sent on their way by the Holy Spirit, went down to Seleucia and sailed from there to Cyprus.

This was the first mission of Paul and he continued to relate to the church in Antioch – but not in the sense of the un-Biblical concept of covering (discussed in detail in my book "Restoring the Broken Foundations). Paul and Barnabas did their work as instructed and guided by the Spirit. Upon their return to Antioch we read in Acts 14:27-28:

On arriving there, they gathered the church together and reported all that God had done through them and how he had opened the door of faith to the Gentiles. And they stayed there a long time with the disciples.

It is important to note that **they reported all that God had done through them to the church.** They did not report back to what some try to read into this passage as "their covering". They were in relationship with the church in Antioch and shared the good news of the mission work with all their fellow believers. **The key issue is that they did their work under the guidance of the Spirit. They were sent by the Spirit and moved under the direction of the Spirit. The word "apostle" literally means "one who is sent on a mission".** As Apostles they were sent forth by the Spirit and worked under the Spirit. This is very clearly illustrated by the history recorded in Acts 16:6-12:

Paul and his companions traveled throughout the region of Phrygia and Galatia, having been kept by the Holy Spirit from preaching the word in the province of Asia. When they _came to the border of Mysia, they tried to enter Bithynia, but the Spirit of Jesus would not allow them to. So, they passed by Mysia and went down to Troas. During the night Paul had a vision of a man of Macedonia standing and begging him, "Come over to Macedonia and help us." After Paul had seen the vision, we got ready at once to leave for Macedonia, concluding that God had called us to preach the gospel to them._

From Troas we put out to sea and sailed straight for Samothrace, and the next day on to Neapolis. From there we traveled to Philippi, a Roman colony and the leading city of that district of Macedonia. And we stayed there several days.

Led by the Spirit Paul laid many church foundations and signs and miracles confirmed his ministry as apostle. In his own words in Romans 15:17-22:

Therefore, I glory in Christ Jesus in my service to God. I will not venture to speak of anything except what Christ has accomplished through me in leading the Gentiles to obey God by what I have said and done - by the power of signs and miracles, through the power of the Spirit. So, from Jerusalem all the way around to Illyricum, I have fully proclaimed the gospel of Christ. It has always been my ambition to preach the gospel where Christ was not known, so that I would not be building on someone else's foundation. Rather, as it is written:

> _"Those who were not told about him will see, and those who have not heard will understand."_

This is why I have often been hindered from coming to you.

To the Corinthians where Paul said he laid the foundations of the church, he wrote in 2 Corinthians 12:12:

The things that mark an apostle - signs, wonders and miracles - were done among you with great perseverance.

It is important to note the things that mark an apostle and confirm the call to apostleship. As Paul wrote his apostolic ministry was confirmed by signs, wonders and miracles. However, it is equally important to note that these were done with great perseverance! He paid a price to do the work of ministry. He walked in great authority, yet suffered greatly for the sake of the gospel. In defense of his apostleship he wrote to the Corinthians and compared himself with others who claimed to be apostles, but were not, in the words of 2 Corinthians 11:13-33:

For such men are false apostles, deceitful workmen, masquerading as apostles of Christ. And no wonder, for Satan himself masquerades as an angel of light. It is not surprising, then, if his servants masquerade as servants of righteousness. Their end will be what their actions deserve.

I repeat: Let no one take me for a fool. But if you do, then receive me just as you would a fool, so that I may do a little boasting. In this self-confident boasting I am not talking as the Lord would, but as a fool. Since many are boasting in the way the world does, I too will boast. You gladly put up with fools since you are so wise! In fact, you even put up with anyone who enslaves you or exploits you or takes advantage of you or pushes himself forward or slaps you in the face. To my shame I admit that we were too weak for that!

What anyone else dares to boast about - I am speaking as a fool - I also dare to boast about. Are they Hebrews? So am I. Are they Israelites? So am I. Are they Abraham's descendants? So am I. Are they servants of Christ? (I am out of my mind to talk like this.) I am more. <u>I have worked much harder, been in prison more frequently, been flogged more severely, and been exposed to death again and again. Five times I received from the Jews the forty lashes minus one. Three times I was beaten with rods, once I was stoned, three times I was shipwrecked, I spent a night and a day in the open sea, I have been constantly on the move. I have been in danger from rivers, in danger from bandits, in danger from my own countrymen, in danger from Gentiles; in danger in the city, in danger in the country, in danger at sea; and in danger from false brothers. I have labored and toiled and have often gone without sleep; I have known hunger and thirst and have often gone without food; I have been cold and naked. Besides everything else, I face daily the pressure of my concern for all the churches. Who is weak, and I do not feel weak? Who is led into sin, and I do not inwardly burn?</u>

If I must boast, I will boast of the things that show my weakness. The God and Father of the Lord Jesus, who is to be praised forever, knows that I am not lying. In Damascus the governor under King Aretas had the city of the Damascenes guarded in order to arrest me. But I was lowered in a basket from a window in the wall and slipped through his hands.

Why was Paul willing to go through all of these sufferings? It is even more amazing when we consider the picture of many who take the title "apostle" in our society and where it is often used to denote someone with a big church ruling over many through the concept of "covering". The North American concept is fixated on power, manifested in controlling people and financial resources. This is in sharp contrast to the apostolic ministry of Paul and the key difference is that Paul understood and practiced what Jesus taught: Leadership comes through servant hood. In 2 Corinthians 6:3-10 we read:

We put no stumbling block in anyone's path, so that our ministry will not be discredited. Rather, as servants of God we commend ourselves in every way: in great endurance; in troubles, hardships and distresses; in beatings, imprisonments and riots; in hard work, sleepless nights and hunger; in purity, understanding, patience and kindness; in the Holy Spirit and in sincere love; in truthful speech and in the power of God; with weapons of righteousness in the right hand and in the left; through glory and dishonor, bad report and good report; genuine, yet regarded as impostors; known, yet regarded as unknown; dying, and yet we live on; beaten, and yet not killed; sorrowful, yet always rejoicing; poor, yet making many rich; having nothing, and yet possessing everything.

This is what the church is all about! It is a people called out of the darkness into a lifestyle of service to the world and one another. The apostles are the primary examples of this lifestyle known as The Way. Thus, Paul wrote to the church about walking in The Way and thus bringing glory to God in everything, 1 Corinthians 10:31-11:1:

So, whether you eat or drink or whatever you do, do it all for the glory of God. Do not cause anyone to stumble, whether

Jews, Greeks or the church of God - even as I try to please everybody in every way. <u>For I am not seeking my own good but the good of many, so that they may be saved.</u>

<u>Follow my example, as I follow the example of Christ.</u>

As apostle he walked as a spiritual father setting the example for the church and for those that he mentored. Thus, he wrote to his spiritual son, Timothy in 1 Timothy 4:11-16:

Command and teach these things. <u>Don't let anyone look down on you because you are young, but set an example for the believers in speech, in life, in love, in faith and in purity.</u> Until I come, devote yourself to the public reading of Scripture, to preaching and to teaching. Do not neglect your gift, which was given you through a prophetic message when the body of elders laid their hands on you.

<u>Be diligent in these matters; give yourself wholly to them, so that everyone may see your progress.</u> Watch your life and doctrine closely. Persevere in them, because if you do, you will save both yourself and your hearers.

In the same way he wrote to the church in Corinth and challenged their arrogance. He compared his way of life in which he paid the price to serve them in ministry with their arrogant behavior and attitude in 1 Corinthians 4:8-21:

Already you have all you want! Already you have become rich! You have become kings - and that without us! How I wish that you really had become kings so that we might be kings with you! <u>For it seems to me that God has put us apostles</u>

on display at the end of the procession, like men condemned to die in the arena. We have been made a spectacle to the whole universe, to angels as well as to men. We are fools for Christ, but you are so wise in Christ! We are weak, but you are strong! You are honored, we are dishonored! To this very hour we go hungry and thirsty, we are in rags, we are brutally treated, we are homeless. We work hard with our own hands. When we are cursed, we bless; when we are persecuted, we endure it; when we are slandered, we answer kindly. Up to this moment we have become the scum of the earth, the refuse of the world.

I am not writing this to shame you, but to warn you, as my dear children. Even though you have ten thousand guardians in Christ, you do not have many fathers, for in Christ Jesus I became your father through the gospel. Therefore, I urge you to imitate me. For this reason, I am sending to you Timothy, my son whom I love, who is faithful in the Lord. He will remind you of my way of life in Christ Jesus, which agrees with what I teach everywhere in every church.

Some of you have become arrogant, as if I were not coming to you. But I will come to you very soon, if the Lord is willing, and then I will find out not only how these arrogant people are talking, but what power they have. For the kingdom of God is not a matter of talk but of power. What do you prefer? Shall I come to you with a whip, or in love and with a gentle spirit?

This message is found on page after page in the New Testament. **The heart of the kingdom is The Way. The first and foremost aspect of planting a church is to** share the message of the good news of the Kingdom and how to live as citizens of the Kingdom. The foundations to be laid are the teachings of this Way of life. These teachings are taught first and foremost by setting an example of The Way as the apostle walks it out in servant hood. Jesus Christ is our Apostle and set the example for his followers. He said it in very clear words the very night he was betrayed as he washed his disciples' feet, John 13:12-17:

When he had finished washing their feet, he put on his clothes and returned to his place. "Do you understand what I have done for you?" he asked them. "You call me 'Teacher' and 'Lord,' and rightly so, for that is what I am. Now that I, your Lord and Teacher, have washed your feet, you also should wash one another's feet. <u>I have set you an example that you should do as I have done for you. I tell you the truth, no servant is greater than his master, nor is a messenger greater than the one who sent him. Now that you know these things, you will be blessed if you do them.</u>

Apostles are not recognized by the size of their ministry and organizations in the first place. Many in the church do not recognize most of today's true apostles. Apostles do not care about titles and positions. They simply share the good news of the Kingdom, touch lives and serve without recognition. The churches they plant are not visible in prominent buildings, for they meet in homes for the most part. They equip and release the members of the body to do the work of ministry and lives are dramatically changed in the process. They often work to earn a living as Paul did, so that they can do the work of ministry free of charge where the Spirit sends them. They are servants with a Kingdom vision and they network with others through personal relationship. They are not possessive in any sense of the word, for they understand the principles of the Kingdom. They operate with a tremendous sense of freedom for they truly walk in the Spirit. They attract like-minded people and they invest their lives in equipping and releasing people or work of ministry. They see the potential in people and have a heart for others, because they are people of The Way and recognize Jesus in others. They discern the spiritual gifts in others and stir these up as they lay hands on them. They rarely work alone, for they are always busy raising up leaders.

Apostles have the ability to flow in any of the other five-fold gifts and attract people called and anointed to flow in those gifts. Paul regularly introduced himself as "Paul, an apostle". Yet he also taught extensively and trained others to do the same as we read in 1 Corinthians 4:17:

For this reason, I am sending to you Timothy, my son whom I love, who is faithful in the Lord. He will remind you of my way of life in Christ Jesus, which agrees with what I teach everywhere in every church.

In his own words he met the risen Lord on the way to Damascus and received the call as apostle. This vision never left him and he was driven to reach the Gentiles with the word of the gospel and to evangelize them, as we read in Acts 26:15-18:

'I am Jesus, whom you are persecuting,' the Lord replied. 'Now get up and stand on your feet. I have appeared to you to appoint you as a servant and as a witness of what you have seen of me and what I will show you. I will rescue you from your own people and from the Gentiles. I am sending you to them to open their eyes and turn them from darkness to light, and from the power of Satan to God, so that they may receive forgiveness of sins and a place among those who are sanctified by faith in me.'

In fact, he was such an effective evangelist that it led to the riot in Ephesus and it is very interesting to read the account and note the words of Demetrius, the silver smith in Acts 19:23-26:

About that time there arose a great disturbance about the Way. A silversmith named Demetrius, who made silver shrines of Artemis, brought in no little business for the craftsmen. He called them together, along with the workmen in related trades, and said: "Men, you know we receive a good income from this business. And you see and hear how <u>this fellow Paul has convinced and led astray large numbers of people here in Ephesus and in practically the whole province of Asia.</u> He says that man-made gods are no gods at all.

Paul also moved in prophecy as we read in Acts 27:9-10:

Much time had been lost, and sailing had already become dangerous because by now it was after the Fast. So, Paul warned them, "Men, I can see that our voyage is going to be disastrous and bring great loss to ship and cargo, and to our own lives also."

They did not pay heed to this prophetic warning and faced a shipwreck. Again, Paul spoke prophetically, and this time they paid attention to his words as we read in the book of Acts 27:21-38:

After the men had gone a long time without food, Paul stood up before them and said: "Men, you should have taken my advice not to sail from Crete; then you would have spared yourselves this damage and loss. But now I urge you to keep up your courage, because not one of you will be lost; only the ship will be destroyed. Last night an angel of the God whose I am and whom I serve stood beside me and said, 'Do not be afraid, Paul. You must stand trial before Caesar; and God has graciously given you the lives of all who sail with you.' So, keep up your courage, men, for I have faith in God that it will happen just as he told me. Nevertheless, we must run aground on some island."

On the fourteenth night we were still being driven across the Adriatic Sea, when about midnight the sailors sensed they were approaching land. They took soundings and found that the water was a hundred and twenty feet deep. A short time later they took soundings again and found it was ninety feet deep. Fearing that we would be dashed against the rocks, they dropped four anchors from the stern and prayed for daylight. In an attempt to escape from the ship, the sailors let the lifeboat down into the sea, pretending they were going to lower some anchors from the bow. Then Paul said to the centurion and the soldiers, "Unless these men stay with the ship, you cannot be saved." So, the soldiers cut the ropes that held the lifeboat and let it fall away.

Just before dawn Paul urged them all to eat. "For the last fourteen days," he said, "you have been in constant suspense and have gone without food - you haven't eaten anything. Now I urge you to take some food. You need it to survive. Not one of you will lose a single hair from his head." After he said this, he took some bread and gave thanks to God in front of them all. Then he broke it and began to eat. They were all encouraged and ate some food themselves. Altogether there were 276 of us on board. When they had eaten as much as they wanted, they lightened the ship by throwing the grain into the sea.

As we read the words of Scripture, we also find that Paul had a very strong pastoral anointing. **This is very important to note this, as many who know they have an apostolic anointing seem to believe that it excludes anything pastoral. As we keep our eyes on Jesus, our apostle, and imitate him we cannot but acknowledge that his apostolic mission flowed out of a pastoral heart with compassion. Paul knew this and imitated Christ!** We have already seen how Paul became a spiritual father to the church in Corinth and also to the young Timothy as he mentored him. His pastoral heart is revealed in particular in the words penned in 1 Thessalonians 2:6-14:

<u>As apostles of Christ we could have been a burden to you, but we were gentle among you, like a mother caring for her little children. We loved you so much that we were delighted to share with you not only the gospel of God but our lives as well, because you had become so dear to us.</u> Surely you remember, brothers, our toil and hardship; we worked night and day in

order not to be a burden to anyone while we preached the gospel of God to you.

You are witnesses, and so is God, of how holy, righteous and blameless we were among you who believed. <u>For you know that we dealt with each of you as a father deals with his own children, encouraging, comforting and urging you to live lives worthy of God, who calls you into his kingdom and glory.</u>

And we also thank God continually because, when you received the word of God, which you heard from us, you accepted it not as the word of men, but as it actually is, the word of God, which is at work in you who believe. For you, brothers, became imitators of God's churches in Judea, which are in Christ Jesus.

Let us connect the dots again to get the picture: As apostle Paul moved in every one of the five-fold gifts. As he planted churches, he always had a team with him. This team included other apostles like Barnabas (who was also very pastoral, for we read that his name was actually Joseph, but he got the nickname Barnabas which means "son of encouragement"), prophets like Silas and young men like Timothy that he was mentoring and training. His ministry was largely an itinerant one and even though he had a home base in the church in Antioch, he did not "pastor" that church. He did the work led by the Spirit and even though he related with home base when he could, he was not under their supervision or "covering". He chose to work as tent maker to earn a living when needed, even though he recognized that as apostle he could have expected support from the churches, for he wrote in 1 Corinthians 9:7-18:

Who serves as a soldier at his own expense? Who plants a vineyard and does not eat of its grapes? Who tends a flock and does not drink of the milk? Do I say this merely from a human point of view? Doesn't the Law say the same thing? For it is written in the Law of Moses: "Do not muzzle an ox while it is treading out the grain." Is it about oxen that God is concerned? Surely, he says this for us, doesn't he? Yes, this was written for us, because when the plowman plows and the thresher threshes, they ought to do so in the hope of sharing in the harvest. <u>If we have sown spiritual seed among you, is it too much if we reap a material harvest from you? If others have this right of support from you, shouldn't we have it all the more?</u>

<u>But we did not use this right.</u> On the contrary, we put up with anything rather than hinder the gospel of Christ. Don't you know that those who work in the temple get their food from the temple, and those who serve at the altar share in what is offered on the altar? <u>In the same way, the Lord has commanded that those who preach the gospel should receive their living from the gospel.</u>

<u>But I have not used any of these rights.</u> And I am not writing this in the hope that you will do such things for me. I would rather die than have anyone deprive me of this boast. Yet when I preach the gospel, I cannot boast, for I am compelled to preach. Woe to me if I do not preach the gospel! If I preach voluntarily, I have a reward; if not voluntarily, I am simply discharging the trust committed to me. What then is my

reward? Just this: that in preaching the gospel I may offer it free of charge, and so not make use of my rights in preaching it.

As he continued, he shared the price he had to pay to do this work as a servant. Then we read in 2 Corinthians 12:13-19:

How were you inferior to the other churches, except that I was never a burden to you? Forgive me this wrong!

<u>Now I am ready to visit you for the third time, and I will not be a burden to you, because what I want is not your possessions but you. After all, children should not have to save up for their parents, but parents for their children. So, I will very gladly spend for you everything I have and expend myself as well.</u> If I love you more, will you love me less? Be that as it may, I have not been a burden to you. Yet, crafty fellow that I am, I caught you by trickery! Did I exploit you through any of the men I sent you? I urged Titus to go to you and I sent our brother with him. Titus did not exploit you, did he? Did we not act in the same spirit and follow the same course?

Have you been thinking all along that we have been defending ourselves to you? We have been speaking in the sight of God as those in Christ; and everything we do, dear friends, is for your strengthening.

In everything Paul became a servant and his leadership was that of a servant. He was willing to set aside his rights to serve others and paid the price for being a servant. As the Third Day Church arises the leadership will be a true servant leadership, willing to pay a price

in order to equip and release the saints to do the work of ministry so that the whole body may be built up, until we all reach unity in the faith and in the knowledge of the Son of God and become mature, attaining to the whole measure of the fullness of Christ. (Ephesians 4:13).

The leadership will function in the fullness of the five-fold gifts with apostles setting the example and re-laying the broken foundations of the church. They will for most part be itinerant leaders. It is important to recognize that the gift of pastor is no different in this respect than the other four gifts mentioned in Ephesians 4:12. The task of the pastor is to equip the saints in the churches for their work of pastoring, by teaching and demonstrating the heart of the Lord for the flock. In this the pastor will work and stir up the gifts in the body as a whole and especially in the mature saints recognized as elders and spiritual fathers and mothers in the local church bodies. Likewise, the evangelist will equip the local churches for their ministry to reach the lost. The teacher will equip the members for their ministry to teach the truth and will stir up teaching gifts within the churches. The prophet will equip the people to move in the prophetic and stir up the prophetic and other gifts. The prophet will also give words of guidance to the local leadership and work closely with apostles in laying foundations for new churches and Kingdom ventures including business. The apostles will impart vision and direction to churches and Kingdom ventures and plant new ones, speaking into the churches to guide and advise leaders.

These leaders will relate to the churches and to one another with a true Kingdom vision. This Kingdom vision will be grounded in servant leadership to the churches and to others leaders. It will not be a possessive vision, but one in which others are encouraged in the way Paul did. As I read the book of Acts and the letters in the New Testament it is clear that the apostles worked with one another and encouraged one another. Paul had no problem when Peter and Apollos visited and ministered in Corinth. Paul did not see the Corinthian church as "his church", but accepted that as he planted, others will water the seeds and yet others reap the harvest. They walked in relationship and respected one another without being possessive about their ministry. They were servants to the church at large and to one another. In the same way there was an openness to challenge one another when needed as Paul openly rebuked Peter for hypocrisy when he tried to appease the Judaisers in keeping ceremonial laws (see Galatians 2:11-14).

The above is in sharp contrast to how much of the church in North America functions. Apart from the denominational divisions, there are major divisions within the body of believers who do have an understanding of the new apostolic church arising in this Third Day. The un-Biblical concept of "the Pastor" as the leader or "point man" in the local church "covering" the people has led to the control over the people to the point that believers in our churches would often not even be allowed to have someone like Paul or Apollos visit their homes to minister, unless permission is granted by the local "pope". It is interesting to read how Paul cared about those close to him, without trying to control their lives. He challenged them as he did with the Corinthians, but trusted that they would hear from the Spirit and make their own decisions. When he realized that he would not see the Ephesians again, he met with the elders and warned them to be very vigilant to detect the savage wolves that would come to devour the sheep. In doing this again he trusted the locally accepted mature leaders to oversee the local church. Paul had a remarkable trust that the ordinary people could hear the Spirit and solve the problems they had in the church. Every one of his letters to local churches was addressed to the saints in the church and not to "the pastor" or even the elders. It is only in the letter to the Philippians that he added the overseers as an afterthought when he addressed the church. Obviously, the churches Paul planted functioned differently than most of the churches we know in our society. It is to this that we need to go next as we seek to find what the Third Day Church is all about.

CHURCH IN THE NEW TESTAMENT

As we have seen so far, the New Testament presents a very different picture of church and church leadership than what we seem to believe in our culture. Some would argue that the differences are mostly or exclusively cultural in nature. This is simply not true. The choice facing the church is whether or not we are willing to walk in radical authenticity or not. **Those who choose to be the church rather than be a member of an organization will walk in the power and freedom reserved for the Third Day Church. They will walk in The Way just as they did in the days when Paul and others planted the church as described in the New Testament.**

So how did Paul plant churches? Paul normally started by visiting the local synagogue, e.g. Acts 13:13-15:

From Paphos, Paul and his companions sailed to Perga in Pamphylia, where John left them to return to Jerusalem. From Perga they went on to Pisidian Antioch. On the

Sabbath they entered the synagogue and sat down. After the reading from the Law and the Prophets, the synagogue rulers sent word to them, saying, "Brothers, if you have a message of encouragement for the people, please speak."

Paul as Jew and as learned scholar began the planting of the church by seeking opportunities to speak to those who were familiar with the Scriptures of the Old Testament (as there was no New Testament written yet). They were mostly Jewish, but also included what was known as "God fearing men and women", i.e. Gentiles interested in Judaism. Using the opportunity given to visitors, Paul and his companions would share the good news about the Kingdom of God revealed in Jesus Christ. We find that others did the same, e.g. Apollos as we read in Acts 18:24-28:

Meanwhile a Jew named Apollos, a native of Alexandria, came to Ephesus. He was a learned man, with a thorough knowledge of the Scriptures. He had been instructed in the way of the Lord, and he spoke with great fervor and taught about Jesus accurately, though he knew only the baptism of John. He began to speak boldly in the synagogue. When Priscilla and Aquila heard him, they invited him to their home and explained to him the way of God more adequately.

When Apollos wanted to go to Achaia, the brothers encouraged him and wrote to the disciples there to welcome him. On arriving, he was a great help to those who by grace had believed. For he vigorously refuted the Jews in public debate, proving from the Scriptures that Jesus was the Christ.

They often began by visiting the synagogue to reach a core group from among those who were knowledgeable about the Scriptures. The message they shared was to the point and was about Jesus as the Messiah. It is very important to connect this with the words of Jesus regarding his church recorded in Matthew 16:13-20:

When Jesus came to the region of Caesarea Philippi, he asked his disciples, "Who do people say the Son of Man is?"

They replied, "Some say John the Baptist; others say Elijah; and still others, Jeremiah or one of the prophets."

<u>"But what about you?" he asked. "Who do you say I am?"</u>

<u>Simon Peter answered, "You are the Christ, the Son of the living God."</u>

Jesus replied, "<u>Blessed are you, Simon son of Jonah, for this was not revealed to you by man, but by my Father in heaven. And I tell you that you are Peter, and on this rock, I will build my church, and the gates of Hades will not overcome it. I will give you the keys of the kingdom of heaven; whatever you bind on earth will be bound in heaven, and whatever you loose on earth will be loosed in heaven.</u>" Then he warned his disciples not to tell anyone that he was the Christ.

The only other time Jesus used the term "church" was in Matthew 18:17 where he spoke about the issue of dealing with a brother that sinned against another and how it is to be handled. Directly following that we read in Matthew 18:18:

"I tell you the truth, whatever you bind on earth will be bound in heaven, and whatever you loose on earth will be loosed in heaven."

Thus, Jesus' only words regarding the church first connected the foundations of the church with the recognition that he is the Messiah. This can only happen through divine revelation. Once he is recognized as one sent by the Father, the foundation is in place for the church to be built. That also opened the door for the believer to receive the keys of the kingdom, which is the authority to operate in power – to bind and to lose! This is exactly what Paul and the others did as they shared the message of the Kingdom. They first began with the message of Jesus as the promised Messiah. This message was preached in the local synagogues where the Scriptures and promises about the Messiah were known. However, they also moved in the power of the Spirit and this was particularly effective where people did not know the Scriptures, e.g. Acts 13:6-12:

They traveled through the whole island until they came to Paphos. There they met a Jewish sorcerer and false prophet named Bar-Jesus, who was an attendant of the proconsul, Sergius Paulus. The proconsul, an intelligent man, sent for Barnabas and Saul because he wanted to hear the word of God. But Elymas the sorcerer (for that is what his name means) opposed them and tried to turn the proconsul from the faith. <u>Then Saul, who was also called Paul, filled with the Holy Spirit, looked straight at Elymas and said, "You are a child of the devil and an enemy of everything that is right!</u>

You are full of all kinds of deceit and trickery. Will you never stop perverting the right ways of the Lord? Now the hand of the Lord is against you. You are going to be blind, and for a time you will be unable to see the light of the sun."

Immediately mist and darkness came over him, and he groped about, seeking someone to lead him by the hand. When the proconsul saw what had happened, he believed, for he was amazed at the teaching about the Lord.

The pattern of preaching that Jesus is the Messiah and moving in power was the basis of planting the church. This is exactly in line with what the risen Lord Jesus said to his disciples in Mark 16:15-20:

He said to them, "Go into all the world and preach the good news to all creation. Whoever believes and is baptized will be saved, but whoever does not believe will be condemned. And these signs will accompany those who believe: In my name they will drive out demons; they will speak in new tongues; they will pick up snakes with their hands; and when they drink deadly poison, it will not hurt them at all; they will place their hands on sick people, and they will get well."

After the Lord Jesus had spoken to them, he was taken up into heaven and he sat at the right hand of God. Then the disciples went out and preached everywhere, and the Lord worked with them and confirmed his word by the signs that accompanied it.

This again is precisely what we find as we follow the story of the early church in the Book of Acts, e.g. Acts 14:1-7:

At Iconium Paul and Barnabas went as usual into the Jewish synagogue. There they spoke so effectively that a great number of Jews and Gentiles believed. *But the Jews who refused to believe stirred up the Gentiles and poisoned their minds against the brothers.* *So, Paul and Barnabas spent considerable time there, speaking boldly for the Lord, who confirmed the message of his grace by enabling them to do miraculous signs and wonders.* *The people of the city were divided; some sided with the Jews, others with the apostles. There was a plot afoot among the Gentiles and Jews, together with their leaders, to mistreat them and stone them. But they found out about it and fled to the Lycaonian cities of Lystra and Derbe and to the surrounding country, where they continued to preach the good news.*

It is very interesting to note the effect of this strategy as illustrated in the story above. The preaching of the message and its demonstration in power led some to faith and they became part of the church, while others resisted and often persecuted the believers. Persecution came from the religious Jewish establishment on the one hand, but also from the unbelieving Gentiles, e.g. in Ephesus where the silver smiths led the riot as they were losing business from the sale of idols as many became believers. The persecution simply helped the spread of the gospel for it forced the believers to move to other regions and where they went, they preached and demonstrated The Way.

There is something else to note that is very important. As we see Paul and others often started in the synagogue, but invariably they were forced out of the religious buildings.

For centuries the church grew and flourished amidst persecution without temples and church buildings. This was prophetically seen on the day of Pentecost when the church was birthed in Jerusalem. The disciples spent 10 days in prayer in the upper room and then the Holy Spirit filled them. Empowered by the Spirit they moved out of the upper room and 3,000 were added as Peter preached and the believers shared the message in different languages. The church was birthed outside on the streets of Jerusalem. For a while they met within the temple, but as they did not move from Jerusalem beyond Samaria and to the ends of the earth, God used persecution to force them out of their comfort zones. In time the temple was destroyed and the believers walked in The Way without the need of a religious building. Thus, Paul wrote in 1 Corinthians 3:8-17:

For we are God's fellow workers; you are God's field, God's building.

By the grace God has given me, I laid a foundation as an expert builder, and someone else is building on it. But each one should be careful how he builds. For no one can lay any foundation other than the one already laid, which is Jesus Christ. If any man builds on this foundation using gold, silver, costly stones, wood, hay or straw, his work will be shown for what it is, because the Day will bring it to light. It will be revealed with fire, and the fire will test the quality of each man's work. If what he has built survives, he will receive his reward. If it is burned up, he will suffer loss; he himself will be saved, but only as one escaping through the flames.

Don't you know that you yourselves are God's temple and that God's Spirit lives in you? If anyone destroys God's temple, God will destroy him; for God's temple is sacred, and you are that temple.

Later he wrote to the church again, in 2 Corinthians 6:16:

For we are the temple of the living God. As God has said: "I will live with them and walk among them, and I will be their God, and they will be my people."

In short, the churches were planted in a very simple way. They shared the message of Jesus as Messiah and where he was accepted as Lord, the foundation of the church was in place. Upon this foundation they built by teaching the new believers to live by faith as they walk in The Way. This walk of faith called The Way flowed out of a relationship with Jesus, which opened the door for a life in the Spirit for every believer. They were taught about the Spirit and received the baptism of the Spirit. Every believer could receive the Spirit and hear the voice of God. The Way is nothing else than living and walking in the Spirit. As Peter wrote in 2 Peter 1:1-11:

Simon Peter, a servant and apostle of Jesus Christ, to those who through the righteousness of our God and Savior Jesus Christ have received a faith as precious as ours:

Grace and peace be yours in abundance through the knowledge of God and of Jesus our Lord.

His divine power has given us everything we need for life and godliness through our knowledge of him who called us by his own glory and goodness. Through these he has given us his very great and precious promises, so that through them you may participate in the divine nature and escape the corruption in the world caused by evil desires.

For this very reason, make every effort to add to your faith goodness; and to goodness, knowledge; and to knowledge, self-control; and to self-control, perseverance; and to perseverance, godliness; and to godliness, brotherly kindness; and to brotherly kindness, love. For if you possess these qualities in increasing measure, they will keep you from being ineffective and unproductive in your knowledge of our Lord Jesus Christ. But if anyone does not have them, he is nearsighted and blind, and has forgotten that he has been cleansed from his past sins.

Therefore, my brothers, be all the more eager to make your calling and election sure. For if you do these things, you will never fall, and you will receive a rich welcome into the eternal kingdom of our Lord and Savior Jesus Christ.

The church was planted where people accepted Jesus as Lord and were filled with the Spirit. They walked in The Way as they exercised this faith in everyday life situations. Growing in the faith meant that they became more effective and productive in the knowledge of the Lord Jesus Christ. Their lives became fruitful and they touched and transformed other lives. Planting the church in the times of the New Testament had nothing to do with buildings and programs and ordained clergy to manage and oversee the ministry! **The church is nothing else than God's people and where two or three are gathered in his name, he is present with them.**

The early believers met together on a regular basis. They did not have special buildings called churches and the expenses to keep such buildings, for they met together for thee most part in local homes. We find references to this throughout the New Testament, e.g.

<u>Romans 16:3-5:</u>
Greet Priscilla and Aquila, my fellow workers in Christ Jesus. They risked their lives for me. Not only I but all the churches of the Gentiles are grateful to them. Greet also the church that meets at their house.

<u>1 Corinthians 16:19:</u>
The churches in the province of Asia send you greetings. Aquila and Priscilla greet you warmly in the Lord, and so does the church that meets at their house.

<u>Colossians 4:15:</u>
Give my greetings to the brothers at Laodicea, and to Nympha and the church in her house.

<u>Philemon 1-2:</u>
To Philemon our dear friend and fellow worker, to Apphia our sister, to Archippus our fellow soldier and to the church that meets in your home:

It is very important to note the terminology in these references. It is not the cell group or the small group that meets at the house. It is not a part of the church. **They knew that where God's people are gathered the church is. Period! Also note that nowhere do we find a reference to "the Pastor". The church is simply God's people gathering in the name of the risen Lord, Jesus Christ.**

What did they do when they gathered? Let us seek the dots in Scripture to complete this picture. We begin with Acts 2:42-3:1:

<u>They devoted themselves to the apostles' teaching and to the fellowship, to the breaking of bread and to prayer.</u> Everyone was filled with awe, and many wonders and miraculous signs were done by the apostles. All the believers were together and had everything in common. Selling their possessions and goods, they gave to anyone as he had need. Every day they continued to meet together in the temple courts. <u>They broke bread in their homes and ate together with glad and sincere hearts, praising God and enjoying the favor of all the people. And the Lord added to their number daily those who were being saved.</u>

Before we discuss this in more detail, let us also look at 1 Corinthians 14:26-33:

What then shall we say, brothers? <u>When you come together, everyone has a hymn, or a word of instruction, a revelation, a tongue or an interpretation.</u> All of these must be done for the strengthening of the church. If anyone speaks in a tongue, two - or at the most three - should speak, one at a time, and someone must interpret. If there is no interpreter, the

*speaker should keep quiet in the church and speak to himself
and God.*

*Two or three prophets should speak, and the others should
weigh carefully what is said. And if a revelation comes to
someone who is sitting down, the first speaker should stop.
For you can all prophesy in turn so that everyone may be
instructed and encouraged. The spirits of prophets are subject
to the control of prophets. For God is not a God of disorder
but of peace.*

It is not difficult to understand these words. In simple
terms, all participated and the gifts of the Spirit were
in evidence at these meetings. Notice that everyone
participated. They were not spectators listening to "the
anointed one with the title" preaching and doing the work
of the ministry. They broke bread literally mean they
ate meals together and the meals included the staples of
bread and wine which they used as they remembered the
Lord's death and resurrection and looked forward to his
return. Everything they did was intended to strengthen
the church. Make no mistake; there is no indication that
they felt a need to have a "pastor" to make the meeting
legal or accepted. When the prophetic word was spoken,
they did not have to submit that to the leadership first
before it could be spoken. There was no "anointed"
leadership team appointed to weigh the prophetic words.
The body of believers weighed them. They also did not
see the home church as anything less than church. They
did not sense that they needed to gather separately with
others in a bigger building with a sign on the front lawn to

experience real church with a pastor and a program. They did not think of themselves as a home cell. They were the church that met at the home!

What about those given to the church as five-fold gifts? How did they function in the picture? As the church started as recorded in the book of Acts, we find that the apostles were the leaders as expected. They were trained by Jesus himself and were the primary spokesmen for the emerging church. As noted above, the church in Jerusalem was the first church and primarily Jewish. Their close ties to Judaism and the temple hindered the spread of the gospel until the persecution following the death of Stephen as recorded in Acts 8:1-4:

On that day a great persecution broke out against the church at Jerusalem, and all except the apostles were scattered throughout Judea and Samaria. Godly men buried Stephen and mourned deeply for him. But Saul began to destroy the church. Going from house to house, he dragged off men and women and put them in prison. Those who had been scattered preached the word wherever they went.

It is very interesting to note that Saul (later known as Paul) went from house to house in his search for believers – for the believers met in homes. As the persecution spread, so did the message of the Kingdom for the believers continued to preach the message. Ordinary people were doing the work of ministry and preaching. One such man was Philip and we read of the powerful ministry done by this man in Acts 8:5-13:

Philip went down to a city in Samaria and proclaimed the Christ there. When the crowds heard Philip and saw the miraculous signs he did, they all paid close attention to what he said. With shrieks, evil spirits came out of many, and many paralytics and cripples were healed. So, there was great joy in that city.

Now for some time a man named Simon had practiced sorcery in the city and amazed all the people of Samaria. He boasted that he was someone great, and all the people, both high and low, gave him their attention and exclaimed, "This man is the divine power known as the Great Power." They followed him because he had amazed them for a long time with his magic. But when they believed Philip as he preached the good news of the kingdom of God and the name of Jesus Christ, they were baptized, both men and women. Simon himself believed and was baptized. And he followed Philip everywhere, astonished by the great signs and miracles he saw.

The success of Philip's ministry became known in Jerusalem as we read in Acts 8:14-17:

When the apostles in Jerusalem heard that Samaria had accepted the word of God, they sent Peter and John to them. When they arrived, they prayed for them that they might receive the Holy Spirit, because the Holy Spirit had not yet come upon any of them; they had simply been baptized into the name of the Lord Jesus. Then Peter and John placed their hands on them, and they received the Holy Spirit.

The passage above illustrates how the apostles joined with the evangelist to ensure that the foundations of the church in Samaria were properly laid. They joined in the ministry without placing restrictions on Philip and sealed the work through their anointing. As the story concludes we find that they returned to Jerusalem and on the way back they preached in many other towns in Samaria.

As Peter was led to minister to the Greek community, the message spread to the Gentiles. Then we read how the church at Antioch got started in Acts 11:19-30:

Now those who had been scattered by the persecution in connection with Stephen traveled as far as Phoenicia, Cyprus and Antioch, telling the message only to Jews. Some of them, however, men from Cyprus and Cyrene, went to Antioch and began to speak to Greeks also, telling them the good news about the Lord Jesus. The Lord's hand was with them, and a great number of people believed and turned to the Lord.

News of this reached the ears of the church at Jerusalem, and they sent Barnabas to Antioch. When he arrived and saw the evidence of the grace of God, he was glad and encouraged them all to remain true to the Lord with all their hearts. He was a good man, full of the Holy Spirit and faith, and a great number of people were brought to the Lord.

Then Barnabas went to Tarsus to look for Saul, and when he found him, he brought him to Antioch. So, for a whole year Barnabas and Saul met with the church and taught great numbers of people. The disciples were called Christians first at Antioch.

During this time some prophets came down from Jerusalem to Antioch. One of them, named Agabus, stood up and through the Spirit predicted that a severe famine would spread over the entire Roman world. (This happened during the reign of Claudius.) The disciples, each according to his ability, decided to provide help for the brothers living in Judea. This they did, sending their gift to the elders by Barnabas and Saul.

Again, the message was spread through ordinary people as they traveled. Just as it happened earlier with the Samaritans, word reached the church in Jerusalem and they sent the apostle Barnabus to Antioch. He came alongside the believers to help them to lay the foundation of the church. Barnabas then brought Paul on board to help him and they laid the foundations while teaching there for a year. Then prophets came from Jerusalem to join the team and Agabus' prophetic warning opened the door for support for those in need during the famine.

Note that in these situations both the apostles and the prophets were itinerant and came alongside the church where needed. There was interaction between the churches. They walked in relationship with apostles and prophets and the believers welcomed them as leaders. As we follow the history of the church in Antioch, we read how the fivefold gifts worked together in Acts 13:1-4:

In the church at Antioch there were prophets and teachers: Barnabas, Simeon called Niger, Lucius of Cyrene, Manaen (who had been brought up with Herod the tetrarch) and

Saul. While they were worshiping the Lord and fasting, the Holy Spirit said, "Set apart for me Barnabas and Saul for the work to which I have called them." So, after they had fasted and prayed, they placed their hands on them and sent them off.

The two of them, sent on their way by the Holy Spirit, went down to Seleucia and sailed from there to Cyprus.

The church in Antioch became a true apostolic center and under direction of the Holy Spirit those called to the five-fold offices laid hands on Paul and Barnabas to sent them on their mission. Following the successful completion of the mission we read in Acts 14:26-28:

From Attalia they sailed back to Antioch, where they had been committed to the grace of God for the work they had now completed. On arriving there, they gathered the church together and reported all that God had done through them and how he had opened the door of faith to the Gentiles. And they stayed there a long time with the disciples.

The church in Antioch was an apostolic center where those called to the five- fold offices spent time and from where they were sent on their missions. They walked in relationship with this church and reported to the church what God had done through them. It is important to note that they called the church together, for they reported to the whole church. This is an example of servant leadership. In turn the church served these leaders by providing a place where they could rest between missions to be refreshed and to be sent forth again. As the story continues a problem arose as believers from Judea visited Antioch and tried to convince the Gentiles they need to be circumcised for salvation in addition to faith in Christ. Paul and Barnabas with other believers were sent to Jerusalem and an apostolic gathering was convened to resolve the issue. Once a decision was made, a letter was drafted and Paul and Barnabas returned with Judas and Silas, representing the church in Jerusalem, accompanying them to confirm the decision. The matter was thus concluded as we read in Acts 15:30-35:

The men were sent off and went down to Antioch, where they gathered the church together and delivered the letter. The people read it and were glad for its encouraging message. Judas and Silas, who themselves were prophets, said much to encourage and strengthen the brothers. After spending some time there, they were sent off by the brothers with the blessing of peace to return to those who had sent them. But Paul and Barnabas remained in Antioch, where they and many others taught and preached the word of the Lord.

Notice that the whole church was gathered to hear the report and the contents of the letter. It was not a "leadership issue" decided by the "pastors and those in leadership" and announced from the pulpit during announcement time. Further, the visiting leaders from the church in Jerusalem were also prophets and recognized as such. They were given hospitality and when they were to return, they were sent off with a blessing. Thus, issues where potential conflict could arise between regional centers were decisively dealt with in openness and the whole church was included in the process. It is also worth noting that there was a flow of five-fold leaders between the major centers and relationships were open and honest. In fact, this contact between Paul and Silas opened the door for the next phase of Paul's missions, for he and Barnabas had a major difference of opinion as they planned the next mission. In the end Barnabas went one way and Paul and Silas traveled with an apostolic team on the next journey.

One further thing to note is in Acts 15:35 above. Paul and Barnabas stayed for a time in Antioch **where they and many others taught and preached the word of the Lord.** Tie this in with the fact that every so often we read that they "gathered the church together" and we will get the picture. This was not a church organized with a pastor or senior pastor, meeting in a designated building, as North Americans seem to think is the Biblical way. These people met in homes wherever they could and many taught and preached. People like Paul and Barnabas would minister in different homes at different times, as did the other leaders. There was a cross pollination with leaders moving around and being received by the believers in their homes. It was only for special occasions e.g. dealing with major issues affecting everyone that they gathered together in one big meeting. We can also assume that occasionally different home churches would join, especially if a visiting apostle or prophet was passing through. One such reference is found in Acts 20:4-12 where Luke reported:

Paul was accompanied by Sopater son of Pyrrhus from Berea, Aristarchus and Secundus from Thessalonica, Gaius from Derbe, Timothy also, and Tychicus and Trophimus from the province of Asia. These men went on ahead and waited for us at Troas. <u>But we sailed from Philippi after the Feast of Unleavened Bread, and five days later joined the others at Troas, where we stayed seven days.</u>

<u>*On the first day of the week we came together to break bread. Paul spoke to the people and, because he intended to leave the next day, kept on talking until midnight. There were many lamps in the upstairs room where we were meeting. Seated in a window was a young man named Eutychus, who was sinking into a deep sleep as Paul talked on and on. When he was sound asleep, he fell to the ground from the third story and was picked up dead. Paul went down, threw himself on the young man and put his arms around him. "Don't be alarmed," he said. "He's alive!" Then he went upstairs again and broke bread and ate. After talking until daylight, he left. The people took the young man home alive and were greatly comforted.*</u>

As we read the above and the letters throughout the New Testament, we find a picture of apostolic leaders traveling, staying in areas and towns for short to longer periods of time to minister and to plant churches. Many were acknowledged and accepted as gifts of Christ to the church and recognized as apostles, prophets, evangelists, pastors or teachers. They were seldom alone as they usually traveled with a team including others in the five-fold offices and often also younger people being trained and raised up as leaders. These leaders were not the only ones moving around and visiting other churches. Many believers did the same. At times they were sent on a specific mission by leaders such as Paul as we read in Colossians 4:7-9:

Tychicus will tell you all the news about me. He is a dear brother, a faithful minister and fellow servant in the Lord. I am sending him to you for the express purpose that you may know about our circumstances and that he may encourage your hearts. He is coming with Onesimus, our faithful and dear brother, who is one of you. They will tell you everything that is happening here.

It is an amazing picture of relationship and support that unfolds as one reads these accounts. Homes were not just places of meeting for the local believers, but also the welcoming centers for the itinerant ministers, whether they were leaders or not. The gift of hospitality was widely practiced and expected. Hospitality was part and parcel of The Way. It did not matter whether the visiting believer had a special relationship with or was personally known to the church. Paul had no problem writing a letter to the Colossians, even though Epaphras planted that particular church and we have no record at the time that Paul knew them on a personal basis. Likewise, we find Paul writing a letter to the church in Rome and among other things he expected help from them on his way to Spain, even though at the time of writing he had not personally been there, Romans 15:19-33:

So, from Jerusalem all the way around to Illyricum, I have fully proclaimed the gospel of Christ. It has always been my ambition to preach the gospel where Christ was not known, so that I would not be building on someone else's foundation. Rather, as it is written:

"Those who were not told about him will see,

and those who have not heard will understand."

This is why I have often been hindered from coming to you.

But now that there is no more place for me to work in these regions, and since I have been longing for many years to see you, I plan to do so when I go to Spain. I hope to visit you while passing through and to have you assist me on my journey there, after I have enjoyed your company for a while. Now, however, I am on my way to Jerusalem in the service of the saints there. For Macedonia and Achaia were pleased to make a contribution for the poor among the saints in Jerusalem. They were pleased to do it, and indeed they owe it to them. For if the Gentiles have shared in the Jews' spiritual blessings, they owe it to the Jews to share with them their material blessings. _So, after I have completed this task and have made sure that they have received this fruit, I will go to Spain and visit you on the way. I know that when I come to you, I will come in the full measure of the blessing of Christ._

I urge you, brothers, by our Lord Jesus Christ and by the love of the Spirit, to join me in my struggle by praying to God for me. Pray that I may be rescued from the unbelievers in Judea and that my service in Jerusalem may be acceptable to the saints there, so that by God's will I may come to you with *joy and together with you be refreshed. The God of peace be with you all. Amen.*

It is time for us to get the key dots in this picture. The gift of hospitality is a very important gift. It was widely exercised and used in the early church. There is no way one could walk in The Way without the gift of hospitality. Please get the picture in perspective e.g. by looking again at Paul's ministry and the visit to Troas quoted above. Just the names mentioned meant that there were 8 on the team and they were received by the believers in Troas (and obviously where they were traveling before and after that). At times they stayed for long periods of time. Was this hospitality just cultural? It sure was part of the culture, but more importantly is also a gift given to the church and a gift that needs to be practiced. Further, our homes are not to be open only to those we know, for we read in Hebrews 13:1-3:

Keep on loving each other as brothers. Do not forget to entertain strangers, for by so doing some people have entertained angels without knowing it. Remember those in prison as if you were their fellow prisoners, and those who are mistreated as if you yourselves were suffering.

How did they do this? How could they afford this? Is this practical in our day and age? **First and foremost, hospitality and service are not options for believers. These are gifts to be used for the sake of the Kingdom. The believers in the first century walked in The Way. They followed the Lord who was willing to set aside his claims to divinity to become one of us and who**

became poor for our sakes. They followed the man Jesus who came to serve and give his life for them. Those that made the decision to follow him became servants of the King. They understood that they were stewards of the Kingdom possessions. This is why we read in Acts 4:32-37:

All the believers were one in heart and mind. No one claimed that any of his possessions was his own, but they shared everything they had. With great power the apostles continued to testify to the resurrection of the Lord Jesus, and much grace was upon them all. There were no needy persons among them. For from time to time those who owned lands or houses sold them, brought the money from the sales and put it at the apostles' feet, and it was distributed to anyone as he had need. Joseph, a Levite from Cyprus, whom the apostles called Barnabas (which means Son of Encouragement), sold a field he owned and brought the money and put it at the apostles' feet.

This is an important picture to see in perspective as the Third Day Church is arising. Let us look at it from another angle: The church is pictured in Scripture as a building, as the bride of Christ and as **the family of God.** By grace we become members of the family of God. Jesus Christ is our brother who came to reveal the Father to a world in need of restoration of relationships. Being part of this family, we are to live as children led by the Spirit and willing to serve the Father as we read in Romans 8:12-17:

Therefore, brothers, we have an obligation - but it is not to the sinful nature, to live according to it. For if you live according to the sinful nature, you will die; but if by the Spirit you put to death the misdeeds of the body, you will live, because those who are led by the Spirit of God are sons of God. For you did not receive a spirit that makes you a slave again to fear, but you received the Spirit of sonship. And by him we cry, "Abba, Father." The Spirit himself testifies with our spirit that we are God's children. Now if we are children, then we are heirs - heirs of God and co-heirs with Christ, if indeed we share in his sufferings in order that we may also share in his glory.

Part and parcel of our faith is to relate to one another in the church as brothers and sisters. As we relate this to our homes and possessions, we will find the dots to complete this part of the picture. The Third Day church will walk in true relationship with one another and with a Kingdom vision that will seek to open doors for others. Compare that to the current structure where most give a portion of what they consider to be "their possessions or income" to build and maintain big buildings where "the members" meet once a week – and walk out of the meeting not even knowing who sat beside them that day. To overcome the lack of relationship in North American churches all kinds of programs are developed to force superficial relationships that achieve little. Importantly though the programs provide employment for the "assigned pastor" overseeing them. Resources are wasted as the buildings, programs and equipment as well as the staff needed are extremely costly. **All of this simply means a waste of resources and even worse; it only results in the gifts of the Spirit to the believers being buried in the pews!**

This is why the North American church is weak and ineffective.

In the early church it was not just a matter of homes that were open for the sake of the Kingdom. All the resources were available for Kingdom purposes. This is The Way. Jesus said, "I am the Way and the Truth and the Life," and he gave all he had to serve them and set the example. They did not spend money on unnecessary buildings and programs, for they opened their homes and hearts. They did not need "a pastor," for they cared for one another and when they met together needs were met. However, they did give regularly and sacrificially. Their sacrifices and offerings were directed to real people with real needs. The attitude they had is best seen in the special offering taken for those in need during the time of famine in Judea as we read in 2 Corinthians 8:1-21:

And now, brothers, we want you to know about the grace that God has given the Macedonian churches. Out of the most severe trial, their overflowing joy and their extreme poverty welled up in rich generosity. For I testify that they gave as much as they were able, and even beyond their ability. Entirely on their own, they urgently pleaded with us for the privilege of sharing in this service to the saints. And they did not do as we expected, but they gave themselves first to the Lord and then to us in keeping with God's will. So, we urged Titus, since he had earlier made a beginning, to bring also to completion this act of grace on your part. But just as you excel in everything - in faith, in speech, in knowledge, in complete earnestness and in your love for us - see that you also excel in this grace of giving._

I am not commanding you, but I want to test the sincerity of your love by comparing it with the earnestness of others. For you know the grace of our Lord Jesus Christ, that though he was rich, yet for your sakes he became poor, so that you through his poverty might become rich.

And here is my advice about what is best for you in this matter: Last year you were the first not only to give but also to have the desire to do so. Now finish the work, so that your eager willingness to do it may be matched by your completion of it, according to your means. _For if the willingness is there, the gift is acceptable according to what one has, not according to what he does not have._

Our desire is not that others might be relieved while you are hard pressed, but that there might be equality. At the present time your plenty will supply what they need, so that in turn their plenty will supply what you need. Then there will be equality, as it is written: "He who gathered much did not have too much, and he who gathered little did not have too little."

I thank God, who put into the heart of Titus the same concern I have for you. For Titus not only welcomed our appeal, but he is coming to you with much enthusiasm and on his own initiative. And we are sending along with him the brother who is praised by all the churches for his service to the gospel. _What is more, he was chosen by the churches to accompany us as we carry the offering, which we administer in order to honor the Lord himself and to show our eagerness to help. We want to avoid any criticism of the way we administer this liberal gift. For we are taking pains to do what is right, not only in the eyes of the Lord but also in the eyes of men._

This passage of Scripture illustrates the liberal generosity, which characterized those who were known as people of The Way. **The poorest among them pleaded to be included in the process to help to those in need, for they first gave themselves to the Lord and then to the apostles and church.** It is also worth noticing that Paul as apostle did not try to manipulate or enforce the giving by the Corinthians. We never read about tithes as mandatory or expected in the early church. They did not care about a measly 10%, but gave liberally and when needed did not hold back as the example above illustrates. In addition, those who were entrusted with these gifts were very clear that they were accountable to the church and were taking pains to ensure that there would be no criticism in the way these were handled.

We also find that Paul had advised the believers earlier on how to gather this special offering when he wrote in 1 Corinthians 16:1-4:

Now about the collection for God's people: Do what I told the Galatian churches to do. <u>On the first day of every week, each one of you should set aside a sum of money in keeping with his income, saving it up, so that when I come no collections will have to be made. Then, when I arrive, I will give letters of introduction to the men you approve and send them with your gift to Jerusalem. If it seems advisable for me to go also, they will accompany me.</u>

This single reference does not imply that they necessarily met on Sundays, although they often did. What is important is that Paul suggested that they establish a regular pattern of raising the funds and that the giving was to be proportionate to their incomes. Further the local believers were to choose the men they would trust to deliver the funds. Again, there was much more trust in the local body to do the work and make the decisions. Further to that, the decisions regarding spending were left to the body of believers. They walked in The Way and were fully capable to decide how, when and where financial needs were to be met. With this they had the freedom to support and bless the visiting apostolic teams and other believers who visited or who needed help on the mission field.

Having said this, it is time to look at how the churches supported such individuals and teams. First and foremost, their homes were open and they housed the apostles and teams. It is interesting to note that in Philippi the church was planted as Lydia opened her home. The first mission into Europe began when Paul had the vision of the Macedonian man asking for help as Luke recorded in Acts 16:8-15:

During the night Paul had a vision of a man of Macedonia standing and begging him, "Come over to Macedonia and help us." After Paul had seen the vision, we got ready at once to leave for Macedonia, concluding that God had called us to preach the gospel to them.

From Troas we put out to sea and sailed straight for Samothrace, and the next day on to Neapolis. From there we traveled to Philippi, a Roman colony and the leading city of that district of Macedonia. And we stayed there several days.

On the Sabbath we went outside the city gate to the river, where we expected to find a place of prayer. We sat down and began to speak to the women who had gathered there. <u>One of those listening was a woman named Lydia, a dealer in purple cloth from the city of Thyatira, who was a worshiper of God. The Lord opened her heart to respond to Paul's message. When she and the members of her household were baptized, she invited us to her home. "If you consider me a believer in the Lord," she said, "come and stay at my house." And she persuaded us.</u>

Do not miss the significance of this story! The first believer on the continent of Europe opened her home to Paul and to the apostolic team that traveled with him. This home provided a base for the team from which to work and establish the church. Following this we find that this church supported Paul and his ministry and when possible sent him gifts. They chose to support him and there was a close partnership between the church in Philippi and Paul, for he wrote in Philippians 1:3-8:

I thank my God every time I remember you. <u>In all my prayers for all of you, I always pray with joy because of your partnership in the gospel from the first day until now</u>, being confident of this, that he who began a good work in you will carry it on to completion until the day of Christ Jesus.

It is right for me to feel this way about all of you, since I have you in my heart; for whether I am in chains or defending and confirming the gospel, all of you share in God's grace with me. God can testify how I long for all of you with the affection of Christ Jesus.

At the end of the letter Paul mentioned a specific gift sent to him and thanked them for this gift. This brief mention gives us an insight into the support Paul received from the churches, for we read in Philippians 4:10-19:

I rejoice greatly in the Lord that at last you have renewed your concern for me. Indeed, you have been concerned, but you had no opportunity to show it. I am not saying this because I am in need, for I have learned to be content whatever the circumstances. I know what it is to be in need, and I know what it is to have plenty. I have learned the secret of being content in any and every situation, whether well fed or hungry, whether living in plenty or in want. I can do everything through him who gives me strength.

Yet it was good of you to share in my troubles. Moreover, as you Philippians know, in the early days of your acquaintance with the gospel, when I set out from Macedonia, not one church shared with me in the matter of giving and receiving, except you only; for even when I was in Thessalonica, you sent me aid again and again when I was in need. Not that I am looking for a gift, but I am looking for what may be credited to your account. I have received full payment and even more; I am amply supplied, now that I have received from Epaphroditus the gifts you sent. They are a fragrant offering, an acceptable sacrifice, pleasing to God. And my God will meet all your needs according to his glorious riches in Christ Jesus.

It seems that this church birthed and nurtured in and through the hospitality of a believer understood the principle of Kingdom stewardship. They chose to support

Paul and through their support opened many doors and helped him in times of need. Also note that Paul did not put demands on them or any of the churches for support. He accepted that such support could be expected, but chose never to demand that as we see from 1 Corinthians 9:1-15:

Am I not free? Am I not an apostle? Have I not seen Jesus our Lord? Are you not the result of my work in the Lord? Even though I may not be an apostle to others, surely, I am to you! For you are the seal of my apostleship in the Lord.

This is my defense to those who sit in judgment on me. Don't we have the right to food and drink? Don't we have the right to take a believing wife along with us, as do the other apostles and the Lord's brothers and Cephas? Or is it only I and Barnabas who must work for a living?

Who serves as a soldier at his own expense? Who plants a vineyard and does not eat of its grapes? Who tends a flock and does not drink of the milk? Do I say this merely from a human point of view? Doesn't the Law say the same thing? For it is written in the Law of Moses: "Do not muzzle an ox while it is treading out the grain." Is it about oxen that God is concerned? Surely, he says this for us, doesn't he? Yes, this was written for us, because when the plowman plows and the thresher threshes, they ought to do so in the hope of sharing in the harvest. If we have sown spiritual seed among you, is it too much if we reap a material harvest from you? If others have this right of support from you, shouldn't we have it all the more?

But we did not use this right. On the contrary, we put up with anything rather than hinder the gospel of Christ. Don't you know that those who work in the temple get their food from the temple, and those who serve at the altar share in what is offered on the altar? In the same way, the Lord has commanded that those who preach the gospel should receive their living from the gospel.

But I have not used any of these rights.

We find that Paul knew that it was right for the itinerant leaders to expect and receive support from the local home churches, particularly where they ministered extensively. He personally chose not to use the right, but rather to work in a secular job at times to meet his needs. He left it open to the churches to make the decisions whether or not they wanted to support him and when they did, he accepted the gifts. However, it would seem that at times some members of the apostolic team worked to provide in the needs, for we read in Acts 18:1-5:

After this, Paul left Athens and went to Corinth. There he met a Jew named Aquila, a native of Pontus, who had recently come from Italy with his wife Priscilla, because Claudius had ordered all the Jews to leave Rome. Paul went to see them, and because he was a tentmaker as they were, he stayed and worked with them. Every Sabbath he reasoned in the synagogue, trying to persuade Jews and Greeks.

When Silas and Timothy came from Macedonia, Paul devoted himself exclusively to preaching, testifying to the Jews that Jesus was the Christ.

It is not stated clearly, but it would seem that Silas and Timothy's arrival enabled Paul to stop working, suggesting that they were bringing in the provision. Paul stayed in Corinth for quite some time, thus there must have been support. However, as we read his letters to the Corinthians, it is obvious that he did not ask for support from them and his needs were met as he and team members worked and through gifts from other churches. It is also clear from the references in 1 Corinthians 9:5 that apostles like Peter and James expected and received support from the churches where they traveled and this support was enough to meet the needs of their families which traveled with them.

When we look at the bigger picture, it becomes clear that the church in the New Testament met in local homes. All believers were actively involved in ministry and when they met, they flowed in the gifts of the Spirit. The local homes also became the centers of activity providing the base for apostolic teams to visit. Itinerant ministers, acknowledged and recognized as operating in the five-fold offices, led these teams. The teams often included younger men and women being trained for leadership. The work of the leaders was to equip the members of the local churches for the work of ministry, which was done by these members. The local churches were never led by an ordained pastor. The local leadership and oversight were in the hands of mature believers accepted by the local church members and often designated as elders through the laying on of hands by apostolic leaders. The local church handled finances as the Spirit led them and they were free to support those leaders that visited and helped to equip them for ministry. Hospitality was a way of life and homes were open to all believers. They cared for one another and met the needs of the poor. The resources were effectively put to use to meet real needs and they were open to giving freely to Kingdom needs. They did not need to devise programs or build churches or have "ordained clergy" to do the work of ministry. Many gave liberally and entrusted great gifts to the apostolic leaders to meet Kingdom needs. They trusted the leaders who walked in relationship and accountability, for they were servant leaders.

Now this picture brings up a very interesting question: What about the church today? If Jesus is truly serious about his church and in the process of perfecting his church in this Third Day, how will that become a reality?

I have stated it openly that I believe that the church is about to be radically changed as never before. The church is entering into a time of major reformation and most of the accepted wineskins we call churches will be ripped wide open. There is going to be a whole lot of shaking, for the Lord said in Hebrews 12:18-29:

You have not come to a mountain that can be touched and that is burning with fire; to darkness, gloom and storm; to a trumpet blast or to such a voice speaking words that those who heard it begged that no further word be spoken to them, because they could not bear what was commanded: "If even an animal touches the mountain, it must be stoned." The sight was so terrifying that Moses said, "I am trembling with fear."

But you have come to Mount Zion, to the heavenly Jerusalem, the city of the living God. You have come to thousands upon thousands of angels in joyful assembly, to the church of the firstborn, whose names are written in heaven. You have come to God, the judge of all men, to the spirits of righteous men made perfect, to Jesus the mediator of a new covenant, and to the sprinkled blood that speaks a better word than the blood of Abel.

See to it that you do not refuse him who speaks. If they did not escape when they refused him who warned them on earth, how much less will we, if we turn away from him who warns us from heaven? <u>At that time his voice shook the earth, but now he has promised, "Once more I will shake not only the earth but also the heavens." The words "once more" indicate the removing of what can be shaken - that is, created things - so that what cannot be shaken may remain.</u>

<u>Therefore, since we are receiving a kingdom that cannot be shaken, let us be thankful, and so worship God acceptably with reverence and awe, for our "God is a consuming fire.</u>

When the dust settles, much of what we accepted as "church" will not be there!

THE REMNANT

*I*t is time to listen closely to the Spirit. It is time to set aside the rationalizations as to why Jesus will not shake the existing Aaronic order and why the new wine will not rip the North American wineskins apart. It is time for the church to be the church and not to play church. It is time for those called to the five-fold ministries to walk in their anointing and equip the members for their ministry. It is time for servant leaders to equip and release God's people and to trust that the Spirit can do a better work of guiding the people than they can! It is time for the Third Day Church to arise, to shine and to be the light of the world again. It is time for believers to be recognized as people of The Way as they walk in a radical authenticity.

As we discern the times and seasons in the Spirit, many pictures come alive again. We are in a time of transition for the church and in a way, it is not unlike the transition from the rule of Saul to the kingdom of David. It is very interesting to read how David started in the court of Saul serving the king, but was forced out. For many years he literally ran for his life, hiding in the wilderness while being hunted by Saul and his army. David was not the only one and in time many others joined him as we read in 1 Samuel 22:1-2:

David left Gath and escaped to the cave of Adullam. When his brothers and his father's household heard about it, they went down to him there. All those who were in distress or in debt or discontented gathered around him, and he became their leader. About four hundred men were with him.

It is interesting that this rag-tag bunch became the core of David's key leaders and many were among what became known as David's mighty men. When we compare this picture with the story of Jesus and the New Testament Church it becomes even more interesting. Let us do that! Jesus Christ, the son of David, had compassion on the people for we read in Matthew 9:35-38:

Jesus went through all the towns and villages, teaching in their synagogues, preaching the good news of the kingdom and healing every disease and sickness. <u>When he saw the crowds, he had compassion on them, because they were harassed and helpless, like sheep without a shepherd.</u> Then he said to his disciples, "The harvest is plentiful but the workers are few. Ask the Lord of the harvest, therefore, to send out workers into his harvest field.

Like his ancestor, David, he had compassion and those around him were not much different from the ones who came to David in the wilderness. Like David he was able to take a rag-tag group of broken men and women and he transformed them and empowered them to overcome Satan and his hosts. In both instances we find that a remnant of broken lives was taken and transformed into powerful vessels that overcame the enemy to establish the Kingdom of God. In both instances this remnant came from the midst of those known as the people of God! Today is not any different and once again there is a remnant of mostly broken and hurting people being gathered from within the ranks of those known as Christians. Many called out as remnant are broken and hurting. The current structure of the church has moved so far away from the foundations laid down in Scripture that it is causing both the sheep and those serving as "pastors" to be hurt and wounded. There is indeed a great harvest and few workers, but in the midst of this the Lord is calling out a remnant to restore the broken foundations and ruins of his church. The walls have been devastated and many a living stone cast aside by the modern-day builders, just like the builders of old who were challenged by Jesus when he told the parable of the tenants in the vineyard and then said, Matthew 21:42-46:

Jesus said to them, "Have you never read in the Scriptures:

> *"'The stone the builders rejected has become*
> *the capstone; the Lord has done this, and it*
> *is marvelous in our eyes'?*

Therefore, I tell you that the kingdom of God will be taken away from you and given to a people who will produce its fruit. He who falls on this stone will be broken to pieces, but he on whom it falls will be crushed."

When the chief priests and the Pharisees heard Jesus' parables, they knew he was talking about them. They looked for a way to arrest him, but they were afraid of the crowd because the people held that he was a prophet.

As we began our journey outside the four walls of the established church structures, we found many a hurting sheep. To be honest, many times they found us, for when you have compassion, the broken and hurting will come to you. This is exactly what Jesus saw when he looked at the crowds as we read in Matthew 9:35-38. A remnant was gathered and trained and then, empowered by the Spirit, these broken and rejected lives were transformed to proclaim the story of the Kingdom. In the words of 1 Peter 2:4-10:

<u>As you come to him, the living Stone - rejected by men but chosen by God and precious to him - you also, like living stones, are being built into a spiritual house to be a holy priesthood, offering spiritual sacrifices acceptable to God through Jesus Christ.</u> For in Scripture it says:

> *"See, I lay a stone in Zion, a chosen and precious cornerstone, and the one who trusts in him will never be put to shame."*

> *Now to you who believe, this stone is precious. But to those who do not believe,*

> *"The stone the builders rejected has become the capstone,"*

and

*"A stone that causes men to stumble and a
rock that makes them fall."*

*They stumble because they disobey the message - which is also
what they were destined for.*

*<u>But you are a chosen people, a royal priesthood, a holy nation,
a people belonging to God, that you may declare the praises of
him who called you out of darkness into his wonderful light.</u>
Once you were not a people, but now you are the people of
God; once you had not received mercy, but now you have
received mercy.*

Today he is again calling out the remnant. Listen carefully
to the words of Hebrews 13:12-14:

*And so Jesus also suffered outside the city gate to make the
people holy through his own blood. <u>Let us, then, go to him
outside the camp, bearing the disgrace he bore.</u> For here we
do not have an enduring city, but we are looking for the city
that is to come.*

I discussed this in detail in the book "Ordinary people
extraordinary royal priests." Let me quote a portion from
the epilogue about this picture:

> "In the church through God's grace
> and mercy we have seen healing and
> deliverance. These are signs for the first
> and second day. Now we are moving into
> the third day and he is setting the stage
> to bring his body to perfection. He will

return for a pure and spotless bride. He is calling forth a remnant to move out of exile and into freedom. He has taken his church past Passover and Pentecost and we are entering the feast of Tabernacles. He is calling forth those who will walk out of the bondage past the gate of fear and intimidation into the wilderness to meet him. He is calling a new generation of deliverers like Moses, to spend time in the wilderness learning to take care of sheep and willing to live in obscurity. He is calling out those who are tired of serving men with titles and robes, even if they have good intentions. He is calling out the No-names willing to pay the price to be perfected and willing to suffer for the Kingdom. He is calling those who have seen the truth and are not willing to be buried in the magnificent graves of ecclesiastical pyramids. God is calling his son put of Egypt.

Let us look at this from another angle. At the first appearance of the Lord God the prophetic spirit of Elijah moved in a man called John the Baptist to prepare the way of the Lord. We read the account in Matthew 3:1-12:

In those days John the Baptist came, preaching in the Desert of Judea and saying, "Repent, for the kingdom of heaven is near." This is he who was spoken of through the prophet Isaiah:

> *"A voice of one calling in the desert,*
>
> *'Prepare the way for the Lord, make straight paths for him.'"*

John's clothes were made of camel's hair, and he had a leather belt around his waist. His food was locusts and wild honey. <u>People went out to him from Jerusalem and all Judea and the whole region of the Jordan. Confessing their sins, they were baptized by him in the Jordan River.</u>

<u>But when he saw many of the Pharisees and Sadducees coming to where he was baptizing, he said to them: "You brood of vipers! Who warned you to flee from the coming wrath? Produce fruit in keeping with repentance. And do not think you can say to yourselves, 'We have Abraham as our father.' I tell you that out of these stones God can raise up children for Abraham. The ax is already at the root of the trees, and every tree that does not produce good fruit will be cut down and thrown into the fire.</u>

<u>I baptize you with water for repentance. But after me will come one who is more powerful than I, whose sandals I am not fit to carry. He will baptize you with the Holy Spirit and with fire. His winnowing fork is in his hand, and he will clear his threshing floor, gathering his wheat into the barn and burning up the chaff with unquenchable fire."</u>

Let us tie these things together in the light of what we have seen so far, for we are approaching the time of his second appearance. In these last days we will see the prophetic spirit of Elijah move in power in many lives to prepare the way of the Lord. There is again a call to repentance, for he is coming for a pure and spotless bride. Out of the most unlikely stones he can raise up children of Abraham and once again the broken and rejected ones are being called out and being made into living stones to be built into his temple. He is returning to find the fruit on the tree. It is time for the harvest and he will clear his threshing floor. In the process there will be a shaking of the grain in the sieve. In fact, it is not unlike the picture of Israel painted in Amos 9:8-15:

Surely the eyes of the Sovereign LORD are on the sinful kingdom. "I will destroy it from the face of the earth - yet I will not totally destroy the house of Jacob," declares the LORD.

"For I will give the command, and I will shake the house of Israel among all the nations as grain is shaken in a sieve, and not a pebble will reach the ground. All the sinners among my people will die by the sword, all those who say, 'Disaster will not overtake or meet us.' In that day I will restore David's fallen tent. I will repair its broken places, restore its ruins, and build it as it used to be, so that they may possess the remnant of Edom and all the nations that bear my name," declares the LORD, who will do these things.

"The days are coming," declares the LORD, "when the reaper will be overtaken by the plowman and the planter by the one treading grapes. New wine will drip from the mountains and flow from all the hills. I will bring back my exiled people Israel; they will rebuild the ruined cities and live in them. They will plant vineyards and drink their wine; they will

make gardens and eat their fruit. I will plant Israel in their own land, never again to be uprooted from the land I have given them," says the LORD your God.

Let us take a little time to look at the key issues in this passage. Many prophetic voices today have heard and spoken forth the restoration of the fallen tabernacle of David. We will look at that in a moment, but first note that the restoration begins with a remnant. The people of God were to be shaken like grain in a sieve at harvest time to get the pure grain separated from the chaff and to remove the stones from the threshing floor. This is part and parcel of the beginning of the end time harvest as the church is being shaken to bring forth the remnant. This leads to the restoration of the fallen tabernacle of David. Following that we find the prophetic declaration of the end time harvest that will be reaped.

It is very important to see this in perspective. As we already observed there are many voices speaking about the restoration of the fallen tabernacle of David. Interestingly enough, this is almost exclusively seen as a restoration of worship in the body of Christ. The idea is that the tabernacle of David in this passage refers to the tent that David erected in Jerusalem to house the ark of the Lord and the worship associated with this move as we read in e.g. 1 Chronicles 16:1-6:

They brought the ark of God and set it inside the tent that David had pitched for it, and they presented burnt offerings and fellowship offerings before God. After David had finished sacrificing the burnt offerings and fellowship offerings, he blessed the people in the name of the LORD. Then he gave a loaf of bread, a cake of dates and a cake of raisins to each Israelite man and woman.

He appointed some of the Levites to minister before the ark of the LORD, to make petition, to give thanks, and to praise the LORD, the God of Israel: Asaph was the chief, Zechariah second, then Jeiel, Shemiramoth, Jehiel, Mattithiah, Eliab, Benaiah, Obed- Edom and Jeiel. They were to play the lyres and harps, Asaph was to sound the cymbals, and Benaiah and Jahaziel the priests were to blow the trumpets regularly before the ark of the covenant of God.

It is tempting to see the reference in Amos 9:11 as referring to the tent erected by David to house the ark of the covenant and the worship associated with this tent, but that is not the key issue. There is much more to it. This is very evident when we look at the Hebrew text, for the words are not the same! The Hebrew word translated as the fallen "tent/tabernacle" of David is never used as a term to refer to the tabernacle that Moses erected or the tent that David erected. This word is the one used to describe the booths erected to celebrate the feast of tabernacles. It refers to a temporary shelter and in the feast of tabernacles was to be a reminder of the journey through the wilderness on the way to the Promised Land. It was also associated with the ingathering of the harvest during the time of this festive celebration. The foundations for the Davidic kingdom were laid when the anointed leader was a fugitive in the wilderness, living in temporary shelters and hiding from the wrath of Saul. It was then that the broken and hurting were gathered and transformed into mighty men that would overcome the enemy and establish the kingdom. **The restoration of the fallen tabernacle of David is the prelude to the great end-time harvest and that is why the prophetic word in Amos 9 continues by picturing the time when sowing and reaping will be a continuous process.**

It is also very obvious that the early believers understood this better than many in the church today. In dealing with the controversial issue whether or not the Gentiles needed to be circumcised, we read the following in Acts 15:6-21:

The apostles and elders met to consider this question. After much discussion, Peter got up and addressed them: "Brothers, you know that some time ago God made a choice among you that the Gentiles might hear from my lips the message of the gospel and believe. God, who knows the heart, showed that he accepted them by giving the Holy Spirit to them, just as he did to us. He made no distinction between us and them, for he purified their hearts by faith. Now then, why do you try to test God by putting on the necks of the disciples a yoke that neither we nor our fathers have been able to bear? No! We believe it is through the grace of our Lord Jesus that we are saved, just as they are."

The whole assembly became silent as they listened to Barnabas and Paul telling about the miraculous signs and wonders God had done among the Gentiles through them. When they finished, James spoke up: "Brothers, listen to me. Simon has described to us how God at first showed his concern by taking from the Gentiles a people for himself. The words of the prophets are in agreement with this, as it is written:

> *'After this I will return and rebuild David's fallen tent.*
>
> *Its ruins I will rebuild, and I will restore it, that the remnant of men may seek the Lord, and all the Gentiles who bear my name, says the Lord, who does these things' that have been known for ages.*

It is my judgment, therefore, that we should not make it difficult for the Gentiles who are turning to God. Instead we should write to them, telling them to abstain from food polluted by idols, from sexual immorality, from the meat of strangled animals and from blood. For Moses has been preached in every city from the earliest times and is read in the synagogues on every Sabbath."

Let us see the picture in proper perspective. The end time harvest will come about as the people of God learn to tabernacle with him. This is the time that the remnant is being called out – a remnant willing to move through the gates of the religious controls of the Aaronic priesthood to learn to live in the wilderness of the world. Just as it happened in the early church, those who move out of the comfort zones of the Aaronic models will become the remnant that touch the world and gather the harvest.

Let us once more read Matthew 9:35-38:

Jesus went through all the towns and villages, teaching in their synagogues, preaching the good news of the kingdom and healing every disease and sickness. When he saw the crowds, he had compassion on them, because they were harassed and helpless, like sheep without a shepherd. Then he said to his disciples, "The harvest is plentiful but the workers are few. Ask the Lord of the harvest, therefore, to send out workers into his harvest field."

Our Lord is calling out a remnant to meet with him in the wilderness of every day life, to learn to look at people through his eyes. Those who hear the voice and respond to the call will rebuild the fallen hut of David. They will learn compassion and how to walk in The Way. In a very real sense this remnant is the answer to the prayer Jesus told the disciples to pray in this passage – they are the workers that will gather in the end-time harvest. They will respond to the needs of people as Jesus did and lives and communities will be changed through their compassion and love. This compassion and love will flow from people whose lives were restored by the grace of the risen Lord. The remnant is the first fruits of the great harvest. They have been through the process on the threshing floor and shaken in the sieve to remove all the chaff and stones. They have been broken on the hard floor of this earth and learned the love and grace of God as they have been restored. Thus, they have become like the Lord and able to see through his eyes to deal with the broken and hurting sheep. Their compassion comes from their own brokenness. They are the ones who are able to see Jesus when he comes to them in the need of others and when they respond the power of the Spirit is released to change lives and circumstances. They walk in The Way all the way even if it takes an extra mile for the sake of one in need.

Let me take you back to a story I shared earlier in the book: the story of my friend John. Three times he was challenged to respond to the personal needs in our lives and failed. It was not unlike the story of Peter who denied Jesus three times. However, there is another story that followed Peter's failures and we find that in John 21. A broken Peter decided to quit the call as fisher of men and returned to Galilee to go back to his old life as fisherman. Unexpectedly he and his friends met the risen Lord just like they did years ago. Returning to the shore after an unsuccessful night on the boats, they saw this stranger waiting on the shore. Just like the first time, he gave directions and as they threw the net out, they found the nests filled with fish. On shore they even found that he had prepared breakfast for them. Then we read a very personal story in John 21:15-19:

When they had finished eating, Jesus said to Simon Peter, "Simon son of John, do you truly love me more than these?"

"Yes, Lord," he said, "you know that I love you."

Jesus said, "<u>Feed my lambs</u>."

Again, Jesus said, "Simon son of John, do you truly love me?"

He answered, "Yes, Lord, you know that I love you."

Jesus said, "<u>Take care of my sheep</u>."

The third time he said to him, "Simon son of John, do you love me?"

Peter was hurt because Jesus asked him the third time, "Do you love me?" He said, "Lord, you know all things; you know that I love you."

Jesus said, "<u>Feed my sheep</u>. I tell you the truth, when you were younger you dressed yourself and went where you wanted; but when you are old you will stretch out your hands, and someone else will dress you and lead you where you do not want to go." Jesus said this to indicate the kind of death by which Peter would glorify God. Then he said to him, "Follow me!"

Meeting the risen Lord on the shore of the Sea of Galilee was the turning point in Peter's life. The brokenness was healed and Peter was restored. Years later this former crusty and rash fisherman wrote two letters. The first was addressed to those scattered throughout a large region, as persecution was part and parcel of the life of these followers of The Way. Near the end of this short letter he wrote the following in 1 Peter 5:1-4:

To the elders among you, I appeal as a fellow elder, a witness of Christ's sufferings and one who also will share in the glory to be revealed: Be shepherds of God's flock that is under your care, serving as overseers - not because you must, but because you are willing, as God wants you to be; not greedy for money, but eager to serve; not lording it over those entrusted to you, but being examples to the flock. And when the Chief Shepherd appears, you will receive the crown of glory that will never fade away.

This tells it all, doesn't it? It really is about displaying and sharing the love of God in Christ with others in a radical way. The Spirit is speaking clearly and calling forth the remnant. It is time for decisions, but before we do, let us look at one further Biblical example of a remnant being called out. In the year 586 BC Jerusalem fell to the Babylonians and many were taken captive to join others that were taken into exile with King Jehoiachin 11 years earlier. The prophetic word promised that a remnant would return. However, when the time came many were comfortably settled in Babylonia and not very eager to leave. Thus, the prophetic call came forth as a challenge in Isaiah 55:1- 3:

Come, all you who are thirsty, come to the waters; and you who have no money, come, buy and eat!

Come, buy wine and milk without money and without cost.

<u>*Why spend money on what is not bread, and your labor on what does not satisfy?*</u>

Listen, listen to me, and eat what is good, and your soul will delight in the richest of fare.

Give ear and come to me; hear me, that your soul may live.

I will make an everlasting covenant with you, my faithful love promised to David.

Not many heeded the call, but in the end a remnant did return and under Nehemiah the walls of the city were rebuilt. Later the foundation of the temple was laid anew and under Zerubbabel it was completed. The seemingly insignificant remnant chose to return and not to spend their money on what was not bread and their labor on what did not satisfy. Today the prophetic call is coming to the church that is again in exile in the very structures it built for itself according to worldly models. This prophetic call is a call to hear the voice of God and to see the lack of fruit produced by the current structures. It is a call to re-evaluate the time and energy spent in unsatisfying labor and the resources wasted in programs and buildings that are not Kingdom focused. It is a challenge to leave all of that behind, to rise up and walk in The Way.

There is also a prophetic promise that is revealed in the old story of the remnant that did heed the call moved back to rebuild and restore the broken foundations. We read the following in Haggai 2:6-9:

"This is what the LORD Almighty says: <u>'In a little while I will once more shake the heavens and the earth, the sea and the dry land. I will shake all nations, and the desired of all nations will come, and I will fill this house with glory,' says the LORD Almighty. 'The silver is mine and the gold is mine,' declares the LORD Almighty. 'The glory of this present house will be greater than the glory of the former house,' says</u>

the LORD Almighty. 'And in this place I will grant peace,' declares the LORD Almighty."

As they invested their lives in the rebuilding of this temple, we read another promise in Zechariah 4:6-10:

"This is the word of the LORD to Zerubbabel: <u>'Not by might nor by power, but by my Spirit,' says the LORD Almighty.</u>

"What are you, O mighty mountain? Before Zerubbabel you will become level ground. Then he will bring out the capstone to shouts of 'God bless it! God bless it!'"

Then the word of the LORD came to me: "The hands of Zerubbabel have laid the foundation of this temple; his hands will also complete it. Then you will know that the LORD Almighty has sent me to you."

"Who despises the day of small things? Men will rejoice when they see the plumb line in the hand of Zerubbabel."

It is time for a decision. It is time to listen to the Spirit. For many years the church in North America has been weak and ineffective. We have spent major resources of time, money and lives to build and maintain buildings and run programs that have not produced kingdom fruit. Many broken and hurting sheep are wandering on the barren hills without a shepherd. When Jesus shows up in the person in need he is not recognized. It is not different from the days when John wrote in the first chapter of his gospel in verses 10-11:

He was in the world, and though the world was made through him, the world did not recognize him. He came to that which was his own, but his own did not receive him.

Those who hear the Spirit and heed the call are as yet a small and seemingly insignificant little group. However, do not despise the day of small things! It is not through power or might, nor through buildings and programs, but through the Spirit. Over 2000 years ago in a barn in Bethlehem, Ephrathah, a little boy was born. Few noticed and fewer yet cared, but the prophetic voice was clear through Micah 5:2-5:

"But you, Bethlehem Ephrathah, though you are small among the clans of Judah, out of you will come for me one who will be ruler over Israel, whose origins are from of old, from ancient times."

Therefore, Israel will be abandoned until the time when she who is in labor gives birth and the rest of his brothers return to join the Israelites.

He will stand and shepherd his flock in the strength of the LORD, in the majesty of the name of the LORD his God.

And they will live securely, for then his greatness will reach to the ends of the earth.

And he will be their peace.

That little one who was born in obscurity changed the entire history of the world and the universe! He is the

Shepherd calling out the remnant to perfect his body, the church, as this Third Day is dawning. It is time for the decision and for the people of God to walk again as they did so many years ago in The Way. It is time for those who are willing to pay the price to be the church and live with a radical authenticity that will bring forth fruit that will last. It is time for the captives to walk in the liberty of the Spirit. Let us therefore go through the gates into the wilderness and be the people we are called to be!

BEING THE CHURCH

As we begin this final chapter, it is important to emphasize that this is specifically for those who are tired of playing church. It is for those who have sensed in their spirit that there is more to the Kingdom than what we find in the North American church. This is specifically for those who are willing to follow the call of the Lord wherever he may lead and who are committed to obedience whatever it may cost. It is for those who are committed to radical authenticity in their faith.

Let us start with a familiar story of a man who walked in this kind of radical authenticity. You know the story well, but listen again to how it began as we read Acts 9:1-9:

Meanwhile, Saul was still breathing out murderous threats against the Lord's disciples. He went to the high priest and asked him for letters to the synagogues in Damascus, so that if he found any there who belonged to the Way, whether men or women, he might take them as prisoners to Jerusalem. As he neared Damascus on his journey, suddenly a light from heaven flashed around him. He fell to the ground and heard a voice say to him, "Saul, Saul, why do you persecute me?"

"Who are you, Lord?" Saul asked.

"I am Jesus, whom you are persecuting," he replied. "Now get up and go into the city, and you will be told what you must do."

The men traveling with Saul stood there speechless; they heard the sound but did not see anyone. Saul got up from the ground, but when he opened his eyes, he could see nothing. So, they led him by the hand into Damascus. For three days he was blind, and did not eat or drink anything.

Following this God spoke to a disciple to go to the house where Paul was and lay hands on him. Ananias was understandably hesitant, but we read in Acts 9:15-23:

But the Lord said to Ananias, "Go! This man is my chosen instrument to carry my name before the Gentiles and their kings and before the people of Israel. I will show him how much he must suffer for my name."

Then Ananias went to the house and entered it. Placing his hands on Saul, he said, "Brother Saul, the Lord - Jesus, who appeared to you on the road as you were coming here - has sent me so that you may see again and be filled with the Holy Spirit." Immediately, something like scales fell from Saul's eyes, and he could see again. He got up and was baptized, and after taking some food, he regained his strength.

Saul spent several days with the disciples in Damascus. At once he began to preach in the synagogues that Jesus is the Son of God. All those who heard him were astonished and asked, "Isn't he the man who raised havoc in Jerusalem among those who call on this name? And hasn't he come here to take them as prisoners to the chief priests?" Yet Saul grew more and more powerful and baffled the Jews living in Damascus by proving that Jesus is the Christ.

The keys to this radical authenticity that became so visible in the life of Paul are found in the story quoted above. First there was the personal encounter with the risen Lord and the surrender to his will. Second there was the empowerment by the Spirit when Ananias placed his hands on Paul. From that day Paul empowered by the Spirit and obedient to the Lord walked in radical authenticity pursuing the vision for his life. In the words he penned in Philippians 3:4-14:

If anyone else thinks he has reasons to put confidence in the flesh, I have more: circumcised on the eighth day, of the people of Israel, of the tribe of Benjamin, a Hebrew of Hebrews; in regard to the law, a Pharisee; as for zeal, persecuting the church; as for legalistic righteousness, faultless.

But whatever was to my profit I now consider loss for the sake of Christ. What is more, I consider everything a loss compared to the surpassing greatness of knowing Christ Jesus my Lord, for whose sake I have lost all things. I consider them rubbish, that I may gain Christ and be found in him, not having a righteousness of my own that comes from the law, but that which is through faith in Christ - the righteousness that comes from God and is by faith. I want to know Christ and the power of his resurrection and the fellowship of sharing in his sufferings, becoming like him in his death, and so, somehow, to attain to the resurrection from the dead.

Not that I have already obtained all this, or have already been made perfect, but I press on to take hold of that for which Christ Jesus took hold of me. Brothers, I do not consider myself yet to have taken hold of it. But one thing I do: Forgetting what is behind and straining toward what is ahead, I press on toward the goal to win the prize for which God has called me heavenward in Christ Jesus.

Years later having paid a very heavy price, he stood as prisoner before King Agrippa and related the story of how he met the risen Lord on the road to Damascus, saying as recorded by Luke in Acts 26:15-23:

"Then I asked, 'Who are you, Lord?'

"'I am Jesus, whom you are persecuting,' the Lord replied. 'Now get up and stand on your feet. I have appeared to you to appoint you as a servant and as a witness of what you have seen of me and what I will show you. I will rescue you from your own people and from the Gentiles. I am sending you to them to open their eyes and turn them from darkness to light, and from the power of Satan to God, so that they may receive forgiveness of sins and a place among those who are sanctified by faith in me.'

So then, King Agrippa, I was not disobedient to the vision from heaven. First to those in Damascus, then to those in Jerusalem and in all Judea, and to the Gentiles also, I preached that they should repent and turn to God and prove their repentance by their deeds. That is why the Jews seized me in the temple courts and tried to kill me. But I have had God's help to this very day, and so I stand here and testify to small and great alike. I am saying nothing beyond what the prophets and Moses said would happen - that the Christ would suffer and, as the first to rise from the dead, would proclaim light to his own people and to the Gentiles."

Paul met Jesus and was filled with the Spirit. His life was transformed and he saw the Kingdom vision and his apostolic call related to that vision. Like the merchant in the parable in Matthew 13:45-6 who sold all he had to get this one pearl, Paul gave everything he had to be obedient to the vision. Radical obedience led to a life of radical authenticity as he walked in The Way as a servant leader. For him to live was Christ and to die gain. He settled the issues of control and possessions, being content whatever the circumstance. He walked in the Spirit and was led by the Spirit. He equipped and released many and planted churches wherever he could. He walked in authority, but never abused or manipulated others or sought his own gain. At the end of his life, from a cold prison cell with winter on the way, he wrote to his spiritual son, Timothy, saying (2 Timothy 4:6-8):

For I am already being poured out like a drink offering, and the time has come for my departure. I have fought the good fight, I have finished the race, I have kept the faith. Now there is in store for me the crown of righteousness, which the

Lord, the righteous Judge, will award to me on that day - and not only to me, but also to all who have longed for his appearing.

Now, let us return to the crucial question about your life. Like Paul, the first step is the encounter with the risen Lord. There is no way around it and your response to the risen Lord's claims upon your life will determine whether you will walk in The Way or not. It is not just accepting Jesus as Savior. He is to be the Lord in your life. With that there is to be a total surrender to his will and an openness to change as his will is revealed in your life in time. It also involves the issue of your possessions for we do not own anything. We came into this world by grace and mercy and live by grace every second of the day. All we have are entrusted to us as stewards to manage for the sake of the Kingdom as directed by the King.

The second part is the recognition that you need the living presence of the Holy Spirit to live this Kingdom lifestyle. Like Paul we cannot see the King or the Kingdom vision without the power and presence of the Spirit. You need to be filled with the Spirit, as The Way is nothing else than walking by the Spirit. The authentic life you are called to live is nothing other than letting the presence of the Spirit be made manifest in everything you do. He will enable you to hear the voice of Jesus and to see the world as Jesus sees. He will set the agenda for your life and guide you in The Way. More importantly, he will reveal Jesus to you and enable you to recognize him in others so that you will not miss the divine appointments set up for you. He will work through you and release gifts that will enable you to do the work of ministry and fulfill your calling. In the words of Peter in 2 Peter 1:2-11:

Grace and peace be yours in abundance through the knowledge of God and of Jesus our Lord.

His divine power has given us everything we need for life and godliness through our knowledge of him who called us by his own glory and goodness. Through these he has given us his very great and precious promises, so that through them you may participate in the divine nature and escape the corruption in the world caused by evil desires.

For this very reason, make every effort to add to your faith goodness; and to goodness, knowledge; and to knowledge, self-control; and to self-control, perseverance; and to perseverance, godliness; and to godliness, brotherly kindness; and to brotherly kindness, love. *For if you possess these qualities in increasing measure, they will keep you from being ineffective and unproductive in your knowledge of our Lord Jesus Christ.* But if anyone does not have them, he is nearsighted and blind, and has forgotten that he has been cleansed from his past sins.

Therefore, my brothers, be all the more eager to make your calling and election sure. For if you do these things, you will never fall, and you will receive a rich welcome into the eternal kingdom of our Lord and Savior Jesus Christ.

It is as simple as this! It really is! His divine power has given you everything you would ever need to live with

radical authenticity, for you have been given access to the divine nature of God through Jesus Christ, empowered by the Holy Spirit. You can grow to become more and more efficient in walking in The Way and thus more effective and productive in your knowledge of Jesus. You can make your call and election sure, so that you can know as Paul did at the end, that you really did complete the race and fulfilled your divine destiny ordained before the creation of the world!

Now the really exciting part: It is not difficult to live this way. It does not involve religious rules and regulations. Let me show you from Scripture itself and this is just a very small selection to prove the point:

2 Corinthians 3:16-18:
But whenever anyone turns to the Lord, the veil is taken away. Now, the Lord is the Spirit, and where the Spirit of the Lord is, there is freedom. And we, who with unveiled faces all reflect the Lord's glory, are being transformed into his likeness with ever-increasing glory, which comes from the Lord, who is the Spirit.

Galatians 5:16-6:1
So, I say, live by the Spirit, and you will not gratify the desires of the sinful nature. For the sinful nature desires what is contrary to the Spirit, and the Spirit what is contrary to the sinful nature. They are in conflict with each other, so that you do not do what you want. But if you are led by the Spirit, you are not under law.

The acts of the sinful nature are obvious: sexual immorality, impurity and debauchery; idolatry and witchcraft; hatred, discord, jealousy, fits of rage, selfish ambition, dissensions, factions and envy; drunkenness, orgies, and the like. I warn you, as I did before, that those who live like this will not inherit the kingdom of God.

But the fruit of the Spirit is love, joy, peace, patience, kindness, goodness, faithfulness, gentleness and self-control. Against such things there is no law. Those who belong to Christ Jesus have crucified the sinful nature with its passions and desires. Since we live by the Spirit, let us keep in step with the Spirit. Let us not become conceited, provoking and envying each other.

This speaks for itself and needs no explanation. In fact, most of the good news of the Kingdom is so simple a child can understand it and Jesus himself rejoiced that the Father revealed the secrets to the little ones and children while the learned did not get it! You do not have to have a degree in theology to walk in The Way and you do not have to be religious either. Listen to Paul (and note how his words tie in with the words from 2 Peter 1 that we read a little while back) in Colossians 2:6-3:1:

So then, just as you received Christ Jesus as Lord, continue to live in him, rooted and built up in him, strengthened in the faith as you were taught, and overflowing with thankfulness. See to it that no one takes you captive through hollow and deceptive philosophy, which depends on human tradition and the basic principles of this world rather than on Christ.

For in Christ all the fullness of the Deity lives in bodily form, and you have been given fullness in Christ, who is the head over every power and authority. In him you were also circumcised, in the putting off of the sinful nature, not with a circumcision done by the hands of men but with the circumcision done by Christ, having been buried with him in baptism and raised with him through your faith in the power of God, who raised him from the dead.

When you were dead in your sins and in the uncircumcision of your sinful nature, God made you alive with Christ. He forgave us all our sins, having canceled the written code, with its regulations, that was against us and that stood opposed to us; he took it away, nailing it to the cross. And having disarmed the powers and authorities, he made a public spectacle of them, triumphing over them by the cross.

Therefore, do not let anyone judge you by what you eat or drink, or with regard to a religious festival, a New Moon celebration or a Sabbath day. These are a shadow of the things that were to come; the reality, however, is found in Christ. Do not let anyone who delights in false humility and the worship of angels disqualify you for the prize. Such a person goes into great detail about what he has seen, and his unspiritual mind puffs him up with idle notions. He has lost connection with the Head, from whom the whole body, supported and held together by its ligaments and sinews, grows as God causes it to grow.

Since you died with Christ to the basic principles of this world, why, as though you still belonged to it, do you submit to its rules: "Do not handle! Do not taste! Do not touch!"? These are all destined to perish with use, because they are based on human commands and teachings. Such regulations indeed have an appearance of wisdom, with their self-imposed worship, their false humility and their harsh treatment of the body, but they lack any value in restraining sensual indulgence.

Did you hear that clearly? Can you see why those early believers made such an impact on their society? They did not have to follow religious rules and regulations, but were set free to live life to the full. They did not have to tithe, for they knew all they had belonged to the King of kings and was entrusted to them for the purpose of the Kingdom. They did not need special buildings to approach their God, for they themselves were the temples and he was with them every second of the day or night wherever they were. They did not need special days and times for religious gatherings, for he was available wherever and whenever and would show up where two or three met in his name. They did not need the services and ministry of a special class of people called priests, for they were all called as royal priests and filled with the Spirit to do the work of ministry.

Can you relate to that? Or does it sound too easy? Listen to Jesus as we read Matthew 11:25-30:

At that time Jesus said, "I praise you, Father, Lord of heaven and earth, because you have hidden these things from the wise and learned, and revealed them to little children. Yes, Father, for this was your good pleasure.

All things have been committed to me by my Father. No one knows the Son except the Father, and no one knows the Father except the Son and those to whom the Son chooses to reveal him.

Come to me, all you who are weary and burdened, and I will give you rest. Take my yoke upon you and learn from me, for I am gentle and humble in heart, and you will find rest for your souls. For my yoke is easy and my burden is light."

Let me ask you again, "Did you hear that?" There is nothing about the many things and expectations so many in the church and in leadership have laid upon your shoulders. In fact, Jesus is asking you to walk away from all of that. He wants to give you rest. Listen to him, for it is his voice you hear. His way is The Way and it is easy and the burden light. He took the heavy load for you and me and carried it all the way so that you and I can be free and live life to the fullest. All you need to do is walk away from all of those religious things and enjoy the presence of Jesus. Seek him and listen to him and trust the Spirit. Jesus said in John 16:13-15:

<u>But when he, the Spirit of truth, comes, he will guide you into all truth.</u> He will not speak on his own; he will speak only what he hears, and he will tell you what is yet to come. He will bring glory to me by taking from what is mine and making it known to you. All that belongs to the Father is mine. That is why I said the Spirit will take from what is mine and make it known to you.

You see, when you listen to the Spirit you can't miss. It is as simple as that. So, learn to hear his voice and be obedient when he speaks. You do not need the permission of any man or woman when God tells you to do something. Just go ahead and do it. That is part of the way. It is good to seek counsel from others and confirmation from those who have learnt to hear his voice clearly, but do not let others make your decisions for you. Learn to hear for yourself. Again, when you hear, be obedient. This was what Peter and John did as we read in Acts 4:18-20:

Then they called them in again and commanded them not to speak or teach at all in the name of Jesus. But Peter and John replied, "Judge for yourselves whether it is right in God's sight to obey you rather than God. For we cannot help speaking about what we have seen and heard."

What about meeting and going to church? Is that not important? Listen very carefully to me and check this out for yourself in the New Testament: Believers have to meet together regularly. That is part of The Way. We read in Hebrews 10:19-25:

Therefore, brothers, since we have confidence to enter the Most Holy Place by the blood of Jesus, by a new and living way opened for us through the curtain, that is, his body, and since we have a great priest over the house of God, let us draw near to God with a sincere heart in full assurance of faith, having our hearts sprinkled to cleanse us from a guilty conscience and having our bodies washed with pure water. Let us hold unswervingly to the hope we profess, for he who promised is faithful. And let us consider how we may spur *one another on toward love and good deeds. <u>Let us not give up meeting together, as some are in the habit of doing, but let us encourage one another - and all the more as you see the Day approaching.</u>*

However, we don't need a special church building in which we meet. We don't need any minister or pastor to lead the meeting and to preach a sermon. We don't need a worship team or an organist to lead worship. We don't need to meet on Sunday morning at a specific hour. We don't need to have children go to Sunday school. We don't need programs. **We don't need these religious things, because we have homes and we all have the Spirit!**

So how do we meet at home? Again – it is very simple, really. The object of the meeting is to join with family (Remember we are brothers and sisters in Christ). When we meet, we also want to have Jesus meet with us. Again, he made it very easy, because he made a promise written for us in Matthew 18:20:

For where two or three come together in my name, there am I with them.

So, all we need to do is come together in his name and expect and trust that he will be there too. Now you may ask, "What do we do when we meet like this?" **Let us state what not to do first: Do not make it North American style church in a home setting!** You do whatever you would do when family and friends visit your home. You visit. You eat and drink. If you are uncertain what to do, just read in the gospels what Jesus did when he visited someone's home! Read what Jesus did when he met with people and expect that he would do the same, but this time in your home through you and the other believers. So, serve the meal and if at all possible, break bread and drink wine in remembrance of Jesus, as he commanded us. Again, you do not need a priest or pastor to break bread and share the communion cup. Check it for yourself; Jesus did not say anything about communion other than we need to do it in remembrance of him.

When you meet together in the house (or wherever – it could be in the field or at a river like the one in Philippi where Paul met Lydia and others first), take time to chat. Take time to listen to others and find out about their lives and needs. Make sure that you encourage one another. Care for one another. Love one another. Pray for one another. (Just read the New Testament and see how often the phrase "one another" is found). In doing this take care to discern the flow of the Spirit. Remember how Jesus was able to see beyond the obvious and pick up deep things. He did that through the Spirit and he has given you the Spirit so that he can work in and through you. Allow others room to use their gifts too and encourage that, for in that way the whole body will work together in unity. Give room for the gifts and encourage the release of all gifts – and do not overlook the importance of the gifts of hospitality and service. In this process please do not forget or exclude the children! There is no junior Holy Spirit and the Father delights in revealing things to the little ones and to those that the world would least expect.

Minister to one another and allow time for ministry. Lay hands on those who are sick and pray for them in the name of Jesus. Expect healings and even miracles. You do not need to travel to a major event for someone to pray for healing. Allow interruptions at times, for they are often the indications of the presence of the Spirit. Again, let the Spirit and the stories of Jesus be your guide. The woman that broke the jar of perfume and sobbed with tears falling down and soaking Jesus' feet messed up Simon's dinner party, but Jesus was not upset by it. He took time to minister to her and used the interruption to teach Simon and the disciples. Talking about that, allow time for stories. Jesus taught more through telling stories than by preaching sermons.

Take time to pray. Remember what Jesus said when he cleansed the temple? His father's house should be a house of prayer for the nations. Allow time for prayer. Don't get super spiritual in the prayers. Be childlike in your faith and expectation and listen to the Spirit as you pray. When you don't know how to pray, let him take over and pray in the Spirit. Speaking about the Spirit, be open to the release of the prophetic word and do not despise prophecy. Encourage these gifts and relax when mistakes are made. Jesus is more than able to fix our mistakes and he already did that on the cross. So, remember to laugh.

Very important: Do not try to do everything we mention every time! Relax and listen to the Spirit. Just ask him to guide you and go with the flow. Do not be too concerned about the structure. The Holy Spirit

is a Spirit of order, but he knows how to bring order himself. His first task was to bring order to the chaos as we read in Genesis 1. Trust him to keep the order and it is easier than you trying to do it.

Do worship and praise! It is powerful and our Lord is worthy to be praised. He promised to be there when we meet in his name so the praise is in order. Rejoice as you worship. Let joy and the fruits of the Spirit be visible in worship and in everything you do. It is good to allow room for offerings and when you give, be generous. Seek the Spirit in how the gifts are to be used and make sure that these truly serve the purposes of the Kingdom. Seek the Spirit in these matters. Don't let your giving be restricted to the meeting, but be open to recognize the Lord in the needs of others. In the words of Jesus when he told the story of the Good Samaritan, "Go and be a neighbor to the person in need!"

This takes us beyond the meeting of believers, for being radically authentic is much more than meeting with other believers. It involves all of life and again there is a very simple key to walking in The Way, as we read in 2 Corinthians 4:5-12:

For we do not preach ourselves, but Jesus Christ as Lord, and ourselves as your servants for Jesus' sake. For God, who said, "Let light shine out of darkness," made his light shine in our hearts to give us the light of the knowledge of the glory of God in the face of Christ.

But we have this treasure in jars of clay to show that this all-surpassing power is from God and not from us. We are hard pressed on every side, but not crushed; perplexed, but not in despair; persecuted, but not abandoned; struck down, but not destroyed. We always carry around in our body the death of Jesus, so that the life of Jesus may also be revealed in our body. For we who are alive are always being given over to death for Jesus' sake, so that his life may be revealed in our mortal body. So then, death is at work in us, but life is at work in you.

In a word: we walk as Jesus did on this earth and we minister as he did. He said to us: "As the Father sent me, so I am sending you!" We are ambassadors for him. We are his body and a temple of the Holy Spirit. Wherever we go, we have to make him known in and through our lives and words and deeds. We view life through Kingdom eyes and with the love of Jesus. In the words of 2 Corinthians 5:16-6:10:

So, from now on we regard no one from a worldly point of view. Though we once regarded Christ in this way, we do so no longer. Therefore, if anyone is in Christ, he is a new creation; the old has gone, the new has come! All this is from God, who reconciled us to himself through Christ and gave us the ministry of reconciliation: that God was reconciling the world to himself in Christ, not counting men's sins against them. And he has committed to us the message of reconciliation. We are therefore Christ's ambassadors, as though God were making his appeal through us. We implore you on Christ's behalf: Be reconciled to God. God made him who had no sin to be sin for us, so that in him we might become the righteousness of God.

As God's fellow workers we urge you not to receive God's grace in vain. For he says,

"In the time of my favor I heard you, and in the day of salvation I helped you."

I tell you, now is the time of God's favor, now is the day of salvation.

<u>*We put no stumbling block in anyone's path, so that our ministry will not be discredited. Rather, as servants of God we commend ourselves in every way*</u>*: in great endurance; in troubles, hardships and distresses; in beatings, imprisonments and riots; in hard work, sleepless nights and hunger; in purity, understanding, patience and kindness; in the Holy Spirit and in sincere love; in truthful speech and in the power of God; with weapons of righteousness in the right hand and in the left; through glory and dishonor, bad report and good report; genuine, yet regarded as impostors; known, yet regarded as unknown; dying, and yet we live on; beaten, and yet not killed; sorrowful, yet always rejoicing; poor, yet making many rich; having nothing, and yet possessing everything.*

We can continue to quote passage after passage in the Bible, but this radical authenticity is nothing else than walking in the Spirit and allowing Jesus Christ to become visible in and through our lives. As we do this the glory of the Lord is revealed, for we reflect the glory of the risen Lord. Where we gather in his name,

he reveals himself. Where we reach out to someone in need, he is served. Where we minister in his name, the Father is glorified and the power of the Spirit is released.

This is what it is all about. Ministry is not reserved for a few select and specially anointed individuals. Every one who accepted Jesus as Lord and sought and received the infilling of the Spirit is called to walk in The Way. When we receive the Spirit, we have all that we need for life and godliness. In addition, the risen Lord gave the gifts of apostle, prophet, evangelist, pastor and teacher to his body to equip the saints for the work of ministry. These are gifts given to the body at large and are by nature itinerant. Their task is to serve the body by equipping and stirring up the gifts of the Spirit.

In the emerging Third Day Church we will see more and more of these itinerant leaders relate to the churches meeting in homes and in other places. They will speak into the lives of individuals and churches, teaching and training the members. They will come alongside the local churches and leadership to encourage and build up these local bodies. At times they will bring correction and discipline, but only to those with whom they have a relationship established through servant leadership. You will recognize them first and foremost by their willingness to be servants and the love they have for the church. You will also recognize them by the Kingdom vision visible in their openness to serve other leaders and to accept other leaders.

It is extremely important to ask the Spirit for the gift of discernment, for as the Third Day Church arises, so will many false apostles and prophets arise as well as evangelists, pastors and teachers. Jesus spoke about this in the Sermon on the Mount as we see in Matthew 7:15-23:

Watch out for false prophets. They come to you in sheep's clothing, but inwardly they are ferocious wolves. By their fruit you will recognize them. Do people pick grapes from thorn bushes, or figs from thistles? Likewise, every good tree bears good fruit, but a bad tree bears bad fruit. A good tree cannot bear bad fruit, and a bad tree cannot bear good fruit. Every tree that does not bear good fruit is cut down and thrown into the fire. Thus, by their fruit you will recognize them. Not everyone who says to me, 'Lord, Lord,' will enter the kingdom of heaven, but only he who does the will of my Father who is in heaven. Many will say to me on that day, 'Lord, Lord, did we not prophesy in your name, and in your name drive out demons and perform many miracles?' Then I will tell them plainly, 'I never knew you. Away from me, you evildoers!'

Later as he was about to die on the cross Jesus spoke again about the last days and among other things said in Matthew 24:24-25:

For false Christs and false prophets will appear and perform great signs and miracles to deceive even the elect - if that were possible. See, I have told you ahead of time.

The apostle John wrote the following in 1 John 4:1-6:

Dear friends, do not believe every spirit, but test the spirits to see whether they are from God, because many false prophets have gone out into the world. This is how you can recognize the Spirit of God: Every spirit that acknowledges that Jesus Christ has come in the flesh is from God, but every spirit that does not acknowledge Jesus is not from God. This is the spirit of the antichrist, which you have heard is coming and even now is already in the world.

You, dear children, are from God and have overcome them, because the one who is in you is greater than the one who is in the world. They are from the world and therefore speak from the viewpoint of the world, and the world listens to them. We are from God, and whoever knows God listens to us; but whoever is not from God does not listen to us. This is how we recognize the Spirit of truth and the spirit of falsehood.

Paul warned the elders from the church in Ephesus in the words of Acts 20:28-31:

Keep watch over yourselves and all the flock of which the Holy Spirit has made you overseers. Be shepherds of the church of God, which he bought with his own blood. I know that after I leave, savage wolves will come in among you and will not spare the flock. Even from your own number men will arise and distort the truth in order to draw away disciples after them. So be on your guard! Remember that for three years I never stopped warning each of you night and day with tears.

On another occasion he wrote to the church in Corinth and said in 2 Corinthians 11:12-21:

And I will keep on doing what I am doing in order to cut the ground from under those who want an opportunity to be considered equal with us in the things they boast about. <u>For such men are false apostles, deceitful workmen, masquerading as apostles of Christ. And no wonder, for Satan himself masquerades as an angel of light. It is not surprising, then, if his servants masquerade as servants of righteousness.</u> Their end will be what their actions deserve.

I repeat: Let no one take me for a fool. But if you do, then receive me just as you would a fool, so that I may do a little boasting. In this self-confident boasting I am not talking as the Lord would, but as a fool. Since many are boasting in the way the world does, I too will boast. You gladly put up with fools since you are so wise! <u>In fact, you even put up with anyone who enslaves you or exploits you or takes advantage of you or pushes himself forward or slaps you in the face. To my shame I admit that we were too weak for that!</u>

We also read about false teachers in 2 Peter 1:21-2:3:

For prophecy never had its origin in the will of man, but men spoke from God as they were carried along by the Holy Spirit.

<u>But there were also false prophets among the people, just as there will be false teachers among you. They will secretly introduce destructive heresies, even denying the sovereign Lord who bought them - bringing swift destruction on themselves. Many will follow their shameful ways and will bring the way of truth into disrepute. In their greed these teachers will exploit you with stories they have made up.</u>

Their condemnation has long been hanging over them, and their destruction has not been sleeping.

As we move into this Third Day we will see and encounter many false leaders, from apostles to prophets and teachers. It is vital to be very discerning. In the passages quoted above we find many ways to help us to discern the false leaders. Jesus said that we would recognize them by their fruit. One of the main characteristics of the false leaders is that they operate with greed. This greed is the root of the much of their ministry. Their focus is very self-centered and they promote "their ministry" above all. They may talk about a kingdom vision, but it is their kingdom "that happens to be Kingdom oriented." One of the dead giveaways is that they like to have others under them, to provide "a protective covering" to their followers. They do not take correction and questioning any aspect of their ministry is not accepted. Those who do ask the hard questions are "rebellious" and are often labeled as Jezebels. When you cross these false teachers, you will be cut off and cast away and even persecuted with vengeance. The loving acceptance can radically change when you question the anointed false leader. **Make no mistake, most of them are very anointed and move in power with charisma.** That is why it is so important to exercise discernment.

One very clear indication is the long-term fruit of the ministry. Many start off on the right track, but drift from the path and miss the call. Watch closely and see how many are equipped and released to do the work of ministry. Watch in particular how long the fruit lasts after they minister in a church. If you see relationships continue to flounder afterwards, it is a clear indication that there is something wrong. If some solid people close to the leaders leave and not continue in relationship with that leader and ministry, be sure there is something out of line. Check the fruit and continue to check the fruit – and do the same with your own ministry.

Exercise discernment, but don't let it turn into suspicion. Practice the gift of hospitality and welcome those sent by the Lord to minister in your church and in your home. Bless them and be open to receive them. Meet their needs and receive the blessings they bring. Walk in relationship with apostolic leaders and churches. Open the door to such leaders to visit and equip the members. When practical meet together with other churches for times of celebration and to allow opportunities to have visiting apostles, prophets, pastors, evangelists or teachers minister and equip the members. Let them lay hands on some and stir up the gifts of the Spirit and seek to receive some of the anointing they carry.

We can continue and find many more ways to walk in The Way and to be the church, but let us get to the key point. Can this model be applied and work in the North American context? Can you and I walk in this radical authenticity and be the church in the same way that the early believers did it in the first century? Were they able to walk in The Way simply because of the difference in culture or is the Biblical model applicable in our cultural environment?

When we started this Chapter, I said it is for those who are tired of playing church and for those who have sensed there is more to the Kingdom of God than the model we have in North America. It is for those who have heard the invitation of Jesus, Matthew 11:28- 12:1:

Come to me, all you who are weary and burdened, and I will give you rest. Take my yoke upon you and learn from me, for I am gentle and humble in heart, and you will find rest for your souls. For my yoke is easy and my burden is light."

The decision is yours! You decide which load you want to carry and which model you want to follow. Your decision will determine whether or not you walk in radical authenticity. By the way, if you listen carefully you will hear his voice, Revelation 3:20:

Here I am! I stand at the door and knock. If anyone hears my voice and opens the door, I will come in and eat with him, and he with me.

Could it be your door? Could you open your home and enjoy the presence of Jesus and his body? It is really easy and it works. It is the way to become radically authentic.

EPILOGUE

*T*his is just a little personal note to those who have a confirmation in the Spirit about the radical message in this book.

First, to those who are wandering and know you are sheep without a shepherd: Simply ask the Lord to direct you to those who are called and gifted to bring healing and restoration. Deal with the issues of forgiveness and release those who offended you and caused hurt and pain. Also, ask the Lord to direct you to those who are walking in The Way and whose homes are open to the Lord. There are more out there than many realize!

Second, to those who have been hurt as they pastored the church according to the North American model: As recommended above, seek the healing and restoration needed and deal with offense. Also ask the Lord to direct you to those who are walking in The Way, especially with five-fold leaders. Also, open your home and pray that the Lord will direct those whom he has chosen to come and fellowship with you.

Third, for those who have sensed the call to start a house church: Open your home and invite people in. Ask God to direct you to the right people and them to you. He is able to set up divine appointments in amazing ways. The key issue: Seek the Lord for the vision and just do it. You do not need man's approval. It is wise to work with true apostolic leaders and seek the Spirit's direction in this.

Very importantly for everyone: Seek divine revelation on relationships. Never be a little island to yourself. In this, do not be fooled by titles or seek big names. Most of the leaders in the Third Day Church are No-names. They are known in the Spirit and will be revealed by the Spirit to those who seek revelation and are open to divine connections. They are often misunderstood and as the Third Day Church arises many in the traditional North American model will persecute them. Those with a vested interest in the status quo have most to lose! However, the truth about the priesthood of the believer will break the traditional wineskin for the latter cannot contain this new wine!

May God bless you as you seek his will for your life and walk in obedience to that will. Persevere and you will become radically authentic in your faith!

ABOUT THE AUTHOR

*D*r. Willie Joubert was born in what was known as Tanganyika in East Africa and grew up on a farm that his parents pioneered after World War 2. It was an amazing childhood growing up in amidst wild animals with no hydro, phones, radios or TVs! When he was 11 they moved to a farm in South Africa. Going to school in the nearby town unbeknownst to him at the time was the fact that one of his classmates in Grade 6 would be his future wife.

Following graduation, he attended the University of Pretoria where he completed a Master's degree in Semitic Languages and a degree in Theology and subsequently a Ph.D. in Old Testament Studies. Dr. Joubert taught Semitic Languages for 7 years at the University of Pretoria before he immigrated to Canada with his wife, Eda, and three children. In Canada he pastored in traditional churches as Presbyterian Minister and then in non-denominational settings, worked in church planting as well as in prayer ministry and applying his faith in business settings and in support of para-church ministries. These journeys led to a re-examining of the Biblical foundations of the Church and a conclusion that the future of the church will necessitate a return to the simplicity of the early church in small home-based churches where ordinary people will do the work of ministry.

With this conviction Willie and Eda pioneered a home church and began to network with others. In the process he wrote a number of books and shared the copies with friends and with anyone interested in these. Recently he decided to formally publish these books so that a wider audience can tap into the resources. "Restoring the broken foundations" was the first in a series reflecting their journey of faith and form the foundation to grasp the concept of the Biblical foundations of the church. It was followed by the book "Ordinary people extraordinary royal priests" with a focus on the priesthood of the believer. This book is the third in the series, exploring the Biblical foundations of being the church in the world. May it too be a blessing to many!